Words for 2 Worship

Words for 2 Worship

Edited by
Diane Zaerr Brenneman

Herald Press

Scottdale, Pennsylvania
Waterloo, Ontario

Library of Congress Cataloging-in-Publication Data
Words for worship 2 / edited by Diane Zaerr Brenneman.
  p. cm.
Includes indexes.
ISBN 978-0-8361-9473-9 (pbk. : alk. paper)
1. Public worship. 2. Church year. 3. Mennonites—Liturgy—Texts.
I. Zaerr Brenneman, Diane, 1960- II. Title: Words for worship two.
BV10.3.W66 2009
264'.09707—dc22

                                              2009016586

Bible text is from the *New Revised Standard Version Bible*, Copyright
© 1989, by the Division of Christian Education of the National Council
of the Churches of Christ in the USA and is used by permission.

WORDS FOR WORSHIP 2
Copyright © 2009 by Herald Press, Scottdale, Pa. 15683
  Published simultaneously in Canada by Herald Press,
  Waterloo, Ont. N2L 6H7. All rights reserved
International Standard Book Number: 978-0-8361-9473-9
Library of Congress Catalog Card Number: 2009016586
Printed in the United States of America
Book design by Merrill Miller and Joshua Byler
Cover by Merrill Miller

14 13 12 11 10 09   10 9 8 7 6 5 4 3 2 1

To order or request information please call 1-800-245-7894 (USA);
1-800-631-6535 (Canada) or visit www.heraldpress.com.

To worship leaders who donate time and energy to working with the words that lead congregations to God.

Thanksgiving   113 - 114

Contents

Note: The numbers indicate entry numbers, not page numbers.

Introduction x
Acronyms and abbreviations xiv

Gathering 1-33

Praising 34-49

Confessing and reconciling 50-75

Praying 76-125
    Prayers of healing 76-80
    Prayers of illumination 81-91
    Prayers of intercession 92-100
    Prayers of petition 101-110
    Prayers and the Trinity 111-116
    Communion prayers and invitations 117-121
    Miscellaneous prayers 122-125

Responding 126-140

Offering 141-153

Sending 154-168

The Christian Year 169-239
    Advent 169-178
    Christmas Eve 179-181

Christmas 182-183
Epiphany 184-187
Transfiguration Sunday 188-191
Ash Wednesday 192-194
Lent 195-203
Holy Week 204-211
Easter 212-220
Ascension Day 221-223
Pentecost 224-232
Trinity Sunday 233-235
All Saints' Day or Eternity Sunday 236-239

Morning and evening **240-250**
Morning 240-247
Evening 248-250

Blessings **251-274**

Laments **275-287**

Dedications **288-296**

Commissioning and releasing **297-307**

Special services **308-321**
Longest Night 308-309
Christmas Eve 310
Ash Wednesday 311-312
Maundy Thursday 313
Good Friday 314-316
Labor Day 317
All Saints' Day or Eternity Sunday 318-319
Intercessory prayer service 320
Evening song and prayer 321

Index for Worship Use .... .322
Topical Index .... .323
Scripture Index .... .324
Contributor Index .... .325
The Editor .... .326

Introduction

This book is primarily for worship leaders and worship planning groups in Mennonite congregations, and for other Christians who find it a helpful resource. Although pastors will find it useful, it is mainly lay leaders and worship planning groups who will turn to these pages for ideas, since they may not have libraries of worship materials and years of experience to draw on.

Whether or not you are a seasoned worship leader, I hope that you will find in these pages sound words that not only reflect biblical, missional, and Mennonite-Anabaptist faith, but also expand the language you use in worship. Most of all I hope that those who worship with these words will be drawn to God and plunged into the fathomless depths of love and joy that we know through our Creator and Lord.

Words for Worship 2 follows in the tradition of the 1996 book, *Words for Worship*, edited by Arlene Mark. Many people have been asking for a second volume—people who rely on the first volume and look forward to contemporary worship resources from an Anabaptist perspective all collected in one new resource.

This volume is filled exclusively with pieces written by Mennonites who submitted their work as a gift for the church gathered in worship. It offers harder-to-find pieces like laments, blessings, dedications, and commissioning liturgies. The book includes sample services for those times in the Christian year not normally covered by other denominational materials: Ash Wednesday, Maundy Thursday, Good Friday, Christmas Eve, and Longest Night.

The goal of this book is to expand the voice of the people in worship, thus increasing their opportunities to connect with God. A number of principles guided this endeavor:

- to use inclusive gender language for both God and people
- to seek fresh, vivid, and concrete language
- to address God only once or twice in each piece
- to connect the divine address with the content of the prayer
- to choose spare, non-repetitive words
- to substitute fresh language for general terms like *salvation* and *discipleship*
- to use *Jesus* in referring to his earthly ministry, and *Christ* for the ascended and risen Lord
- to resist using *God* for the first person of the Trinity, since that title is all inclusive. Alternative suggestions include: Creator, Source, Father/Mother, and Maker.

HOW TO USE THIS BOOK

The book's organization follows principles used in other Mennonite worship materials, such as *Hymnal: A Worship Book.* The worship order used in this book is outlined as follows:

Gathering—call to worship, and invocation prayer
    recognizing God's presence
Praising
Confessing and reconciling
Praying
Proclaiming—Scripture and sermon (not addressed in
    this book)
Responding—including affirmations of faith, sometimes
    used elsewhere in the service
Offering
Sending

Other important worship elements, such as children's time, music, drama, passing the peace, and sharing time are beyond the scope of this book.

It has been said, "Good ritual doesn't love paper." The liturgical elements included here are intended to be more than simple scripts. They should be used flexibly and adapted to fit your context. The following are some hints:

- **Edit, revise, recreate, and adapt the pieces to suit your worship setting.** The contributors to this volume have offered these pieces to be used in congregational worship—either as they are, or as models for other creative resources. Please see copyright restrictions on the copyright page (p. *iv*). When you print a piece (as is or adapted), please include the following credit line in a footnote: "From [or adapted from] *Words for Worship 2*, edited by Diane Zaerr Brenneman, © 2009 by Herald Press, Scottdale, Pa."
- **Use the indexes and the table of contents to uncover the gems of this book.** Let them inspire your spirit to creativity and imagination to lead your people in worship. Note that the indexes are suggestive and not exhaustive. For example, they do not always distinguish clearly between God, Jesus, and the Holy Spirit; if you can't find a piece under *Jesus*, look under *God*. Or if the reference is to the "providence of God," it could well refer to the work of Christ.
- **Browse across sections.** While worship elements have been grouped thematically, some could well have been placed in other parts of the book. For example, the Intercession section (numbers 92 to 100) may include some elements that may fit a service of lament or vice versa. Or the Christian Year section may include gathering and sending material that could be used anytime, not just during the seasonal worship.
- **Vary the responsive readings freely.** Some can be read by the leader alone, or by two leaders, rather than by leader and people. Many, particularly those marked

with numbers, can be read antiphonally, alternating genders, for example, or sides of the congregation.

- **Try teaching the congregation oral responses** so the pieces don't need to be printed (for example, numbers 1, 57, 63, and 101).
- **Build new routines.** Some responses and blessings were originally used repeatedly or weekly (such as numbers 122 or 156).
- **Make worship physical.** In some prayers the body engages us in hearing God's voice in new ways (see numbers 191 and 200).

ACKNOWLEDGMENTS

I owe a debt of gratitude to the willing writers who submitted material for consideration. Contributors are listed at the back of the book. I wish we could have used all the wonderful contributions we received.

The quality of language in these pieces is due largely to the indefatigable editing by consultants to the project: Arlyn Friesen Epp, director of Mennonite Church Canada's Resource Centre; Marlene Kropf, denominational minister of worship with Mennonite Church USA and Associate Professor in Spiritual Formation and Worship at Associated Mennonite Biblical Seminary; project coordinator Eleanor Snyder, director of Faith &Life Resources; and FLR editor Byron Rempel-Burkholder. I also wish to thank Evon Castro, administrative assistant with Mennonite Church USA Executive Leadership for her collation of previously published denominational worship materials for this project.

Finally, I thank my husband Doug for covering my share of the farm work "for the book" and I give hugs and kisses to our kids for sharing mom time with this project.

Diane Zaerr Brenneman
April 2009

Acronyms and Abbreviations

Acronyms for worship resources used in this book

HWB   *Hymnal: A Worship Book*. (Scottdale, PA and Waterloo, ON: Faith & Life Resources, 1992).

MH   *The Mennonite Hymnal*. (Scottdale, PA: Herald Press, 1969).

MM   *Minister's Manual* (Newton, KS: Faith & Life Press, 1998).

STJ   *Sing the Journey*. Hymnal: A Worship Book—Supplement I. (Scottdale, PA and Waterloo, ON: Faith & Life Resources, 2005).

STS   *Sing the Story*. Hymnal: A Worship Book—Supplement II. (Scottdale, PA and Waterloo, ON: Faith & Life Resources, 2007).

Abbreviations used in antiphonal readings and readers theatre

1:    Reader 1, or in antiphonal readings: side 1 or gender 1 (e.g., male voices)

2:    Reader 2, or in antiphonal readings: side 2 or gender 2 (e.g., female voices)

L: Leader

P: **People**

All: *In congregational readings, the whole congregation; in readers theatre, all readers*

Gathering

1 Call to all generations

(involving three generations of readers)

1: Come and worship.
2: Come and worship.
3: Come and worship.
1: If you're short or tall
3: Big or small
2: Young or mature
3: Messy or pure
1: Hot or cool
2: Depressed or secure—
All: *Come and worship.*
2: God is waiting.
1: God is hoping.
3: God is loving.
All: *Come. Come and worship.*

2 Fierce, tender, and abundant

L: We have come to worship you, O God;
P: **gather us in.**
L: Some of us come full of happiness;
P: **gather us in.**
L: Some of us come a little sore from what life brings;
P: **gather us in.**

L: Some of us come indifferent or confused;
P: **gather us in.**
L: We honor you—
　　　who forms us
　　　and calls us each by name.
　　You are our God, known yet unknown,
　　　present here yet everywhere
　　　now and forever.
　　You have made us distinctly unique
　　　and yet part of your people world-wide.
All: *Gather us in to your fierce love, your tender care,*
　　　your abundant grace.
L: We pray in the name of Jesus. Amen.

3 Wake up!

L: Wake up, O [*church name*] Mennonite people!
P: **True evangelical faith cannot lie sleeping.**
　　It clothes the naked, it comforts the sorrowful,
　　It shelters the destitute, it serves those that harm it,
　　It binds up that which is wounded.
　　It has become all things to all people.*
　　(moments of silence for meditation)
All: *Let us rise up in true faith*
　　　and shine the light of Love to the world this day!

4 Seeds and soil

(can be used with "Joyful, joyful" [HWB 71])

L: A dry, lifeless speck
　　　blown by the wind
　　　settles to earth.
P: **Sunlight, soil, rain.**
　　Roots! Shoots! Flowers! Fruit!

*Words in bold are a quote from Menno Simons (1539).

L: Mysterious God,
we marvel at the miracle of new life from seeds.
P: We marvel that your kingdom grows even while we sleep.
L: Scatter your good seed in our hearts this day,
O Spirit of God.
*All: Then let our hearts unfold like flowers before you,
center of unbroken praise!*

5 Privilege of sowing seeds

Come, people of God, and worship the Lord,
for you have been given mercy and grace.
Come, people of God, and praise the name of Jesus,
for you have been given eternal life.
Come, people of God, and receive the Spirit's blessing,
for you have been given the privilege of sowing seeds
for the reign of God.

6 Desire for God

L: Seekers of God, you are here and God is here.
Open your eyes to see anew.
(silence)
Lovers of God, you are here and God is here.
Open your heart to be touched anew.
(silence)
Followers of God, you are here and God is here.
Open your mind to learn anew.
(silence)
People of God, you are here and God is here.
Open yourself to be filled anew.
(silence)

√ **Prayer**

Holy and Gracious God, here and everywhere,
>   you created us with a desire to see you.
>> √ you care for us with a love that softens
>> the hardest places in our hearts.

You impart to us wisdom and knowledge
>   through your law and covenant.

You fill us with your Spirit of grace.

See our open eyes.

Hold close our open hearts.

Teach our open minds.

And fill us with your Spirit. Amen

7 God of glory thunders

(based on Psalm 29)

1: Ascribe to the Lord glory and strength.
2: Worship the Lord in the splendor of God's holiness.
1: The voice of the Lord is over the waters;
2: The God of glory thunders,
1: The voice of the Lord is powerful and majestic;
2: The God of glory strikes with flashes of lightning
     and shakes the desert;
1: In God's temple all cry, "Glory!"
2: The Lord is enthroned as ruler forever.
1: The Lord gives strength to the people;
2: The Lord blesses the people with peace.

8 Praise in the Rubble

(readers theatre for three readers)

All *(in a round, as readers walk toward the front)***:**
> *Rubble and ruin,*
>> *confusion and sin,*
>> *wars and rumors of wars.*

iPods® *and cell phones,*
  video streams **(pause),**
  T-x-t- M-s-s-g **(drawn out),**
  global warming and strained economy.

1: Where is God?

2: Where's the church?

All: *What is real?*

3: Have you not seen it? *(move to the front)*

2: Have you not heard it? *(move to the front)*

1: Have you not *perceived* it? *(move to the front)*

1&2: *Now it springs forth!*

3: Like water in the desert.

All: *Like a strong tree never to be shaken.*

3: And many will come to drink.

1: Many will find shade

2: and shelter.

All: *In the midst of the rubble of the world,*
  God is forming a people, a people of praise.
  A Church!
  Now it springs forth!

9 Hum and dance

(based on Psalm 95)

L: O come, let us sing…

P: and hum and dance and clap our hands!

L: O come, let us make a joyful noise …

P: by shouting and stomping and snapping our fingers!

L: O come, let us sing to the Lord,
  the rock of our salvation!
  Let us come into God's presence with thanksgiving,
    making joyful noises and singing the Lord's praises!
  For great is our God!

P: How great?

L: Very great!
For in God's hands are the depths of the earth
and the heights of the mountains!
The seas are the Lord's, for God is their Creator.
The land is the Lord's, for God's hands formed,
shaped, and blessed the earth!
P: Great is the Lord and greatly to be praised!
L: O come, let us worship,
**P: and bow down and kneel in reverence,
lifting our voices in awe!**
All: Let us sing to God, the rock of our salvation!

10 Trinity gathering

L: Loving God, life of the universe,
P: we gather to worship you.
L: Great Creator, who formed us in your image,
P: we gather to worship you.
L: Holy Redeemer, who became flesh and lived among us,
P: we gather to worship you.
L: Sustaining Spirit, who breathes into us always
the holy breath of life,
All: together we gather to worship you. Amen.

11 Breath of God on the dawn

1: Come, you who are weary from the darkness of the night.
2: Come, you who are hopeful
who listen for the breath of God on the morning dawn.
All: Come and worship the Lord.
1: Come with your gratitude for the blessings of the day.
2: Come with your pleadings for mercy and release.
All: Come and worship the Lord,
1: for the Lord our God is gathering us in,
and Jesus the Christ is our Host.

2: Let us welcome the Spirit that welcomes us here.

All: ***Come and worship the Lord.***

12 Psalm 23

(can be used for Peace Sunday)

L: The Lord is our Shepherd;

P: we shall not want.

L: Come to green pastures

P: where God restores our souls.

L: Come, everyone who suffers, all who fear death,

P: God will comfort us.

L: See, the table is set, even in the midst of our enemies.

**P: God is our host and anoints us with oil.
Our cups overflow.**

L: Surely goodness and mercy are with us every day,

P: and God will welcome and provide for us forever.

13 Rekindle our hope

We long for wholeness.
We hope for joy.
Sometimes both seem to elude us.
The deserts appear to be expanding
and our journey feels lost in the wastelands.
Other times, both peace and joy surprise us;
they rekindle our hope
that things will indeed come to flower.
Today we come with our personal pains and joys—
some of which we share with others
and some of which we hardly dare to mention to God.
But God, who made us, knows us through and through,
and God, who knows us, loves us and wants us whole.
Let us be silent and then let us pray, listen, and speak,
with this God, who is with us! in Jesus!

14 Risk a mystery

It is a risk to have come to worship today.
This is a place where believers
  worship what cannot be seen,
  choose to participate in a living mystery,
  and try—with all of the Spirit's help—
  to allow transformation within their lives,
   the church, and the world.
This is a place where believers try—
  with all of the Spirit's grace—
  to risk letting go of familiar but stubborn ways
  in order to believe, receive, and love anew.

15 Admit we are lost

  L: Only when we admit we are lost
  P: can we be led.
  L: Only when we acknowledge our weakness
  P: can we be given strength.
  L: Only when we are empty
  P: can we be filled.
 All: We are lost. We are weak. We are empty.
  L: Come Lord Jesus, hear our prayer. Amen.

16 One body, one church

  L: We gather as many individuals,
  P: yet we are one body.
  L: We come from many places,
  P: yet we come to one place.
  L: We gather as God's many children,
  P: yet we are one church.

All: *We are one body, in this place,*
         as God's church. Alleluia!

17 Unity

(based on Psalm 133)

L: Let us come together with humility.
P: How good a thing it is when all of God's people
      live together in unity.
L: Though we may be tempted to use harsh words,
      let us come together with gentleness.
P: How good a thing it is when all of God's people
      live together in unity.
L: Though we may want everything to happen quickly,
      let us come together with patience.
P: How good a thing it is when all of God's people
      live together in unity.
L: Though the world around often encourages hate,
      let us come together in love.
P: How good a thing it is when all of God's people
      live together in unity.
L: In humility, gentleness, patience, love, and unity,
All: *let us worship the God who has called us together.*

18 Climb God's mountain

(based on Isaiah 2)

L: In the days to come, the mountain of God's house
      will be established as the highest of the mountains
      and raised above all other hills;
      all nations will stream toward it.
P: Many people will come and say,
      "Come, let us climb God's mountain;
      that we may be instructed in God's ways
      and walk in God's paths."

> **For out of Zion will go forth instruction,**
> > **and the word of God from Jerusalem.**

L: God will judge between the nations,
> > and render decisions for many countries;

P: **They will beat their nuclear bombs into plowshares,**
> > **and their guns into gardening tools;**
> > **nation will not raise weapons against nation,**
> > **and never again will they train for war.**

All: *May we be co-creators with God*
> > *in making that day a reality.*
> > *May it begin today. Let us worship God!*

19 In the midst of uncertain times

L: Here we are Lord, your church, uncertain,
> > on an ever changing journey.

P: **Show us your path.**

L: Here we are, longing to know your way.

P: **Guide us to follow you.**

L: Here we are, desiring only your comfort.

P: **Help us to hear your voice.**

All: *Here we are, God; lead us according to your will.*

20 The love of God

(based on Psalm 9:1-2 and "The love of God" [STJ 44])

L: The love of God is greater far
> > than tongue or pen can ever tell.

P: **Though tongue and pen falter, our hearts overflow.**
> **We long to fill the skies with praise to God.**

L: Then let us give thanks to God with all our hearts.
> Let us tell of all God's wonderful deeds!

All: *We will be glad and exult together.*
> *We will sing praise to the Most High God!*

21 Seeking God's face

L: Come, follow Jesus to the sacred place where God is,
    a place of intimate prayer, of open heart.
P: **We come, seeking God's face,**
    pierced by the power of Love's presence,
    silent before the glory of divine beauty.
L: Come, follow Jesus to a place of community,
    to the place where sons and daughters join as one,
    sharing in the bountiful grace of our Provider.
P: **We come, seeking God's face**
    in our brothers and sisters,
    we worship, work and play,
    sharing our lives together.
ALL: *Jesus, lead us to the Holy One*
     that we might see God's face. Amen.

22 Law of liberty, law of love

1: Creator and still creating God,
2: your creation sings of your greatness.
1: Mighty One most high and yet hidden in the human heart,
2: your presence is our shield and our home.
1: Merciful and gracious Lord,
2: your forgiveness means we too can forgive.
1: Friend of the poor, Caller of the rich,
2: your justice frees those bound
    and liberates the imprisoned.
1: Peace for the frightened, Healing for the wounded,
2: you are Lord of laughter, Lord of tears.
1: Trustworthy and true, hope of the world,
2: you are Lord of the struggle, source of our strength.
1: Perfectly love, eternally light,
2: you hold us like a mother and guide us like a father.

> **All:** *May we know your law of liberty*
> *and live your law of love,*
> *that your will may be done and your glory be known.*
> *Amen.*

23 Straggling to God

(written to follow HWB 662)

While we straggle to your house,
    we find you are already here, ever-present God,
    totally prepared to restore and bless us.
Help us to be truly present
    to receive your gifts of goodness and mercy,
    in the name of Jesus, your Son, our Lord. Amen.

24 Draw us close

Eternal, almighty and trustworthy God,
    draw us to yourself as a mother draws a child
        to her bosom.
Come so close that we know you are listening when we speak,
    so close that you know we are listening when you speak.
Be our hope.
Kindle our faith.
Teach us the way of peace.
For Jesus' sake, Amen.

25 Comfort us. Disturb us.

L: Creating God, we bring to you our praise.
P: **We give thanks for the bounty of earth, sea, and sky.**
L: We hold before you our joy and entrust to you our sorrow.
P: **We are yours and made in your image.**

L: Open us to the movement of your Spirit in and among us.
P: **Comfort us. Disturb us.**
L: Enlighten us. Ignite us.
All: *Continue your creating ways in us and through us,*
that your glory may be comprehended
and your love made visible.
In the name of your Son, our Savior, we pray. Amen.

26 Work and worship

(can be used for a congregational meeting)

L: Gracious and Eternal God,
through Jesus Christ, you have joined us
into one living body.
We thank you for these bonds of love that form us.
P: **Help us to perceive your unseen hand**
in the unfolding of our life together.
Work within and among us.
L: Confront us with your tenderness and set us on fire.
P: **Enable us, by your Spirit, to walk together**
in unity of love and purpose,
to uphold one another by word and example,
and to live in faithful obedience to your will.
L: By the mercy and justice we show one another,
may we reach out to a watching and waiting world.
All: *In our work and worship may your glory be revealed*
and your name praised,
through Jesus Christ our Lord. Amen.

27 A fragment of your spiritual house

(can be used to open a congregational meeting)

Here we are, God,
a small fragment of the spiritual house you are building.

We are your people
    called from darkness into your marvelous light.
Give us light today.
Give us understanding
    as we consider recommendations, make decisions,
    and share in the planning for this congregation.
Illumine our deliberations and discussions.
May we speak clearly, kindly, honestly, and openly.
May we be the kind of stones you can use to build your house.
Through Jesus Christ our foundation, we pray. Amen.

28 Guide our musings

Dear Lord, we come before you eager to praise you,
    ready to set aside our thoughts and musings
        of the week to come.
Guide us into worship
    as we yearn to see, hear and feel
        your presence this hour. Amen.

29 Grow our maturity

for Sundays

Maker of the universe,
    and of the hairs of our heads—
    our Beginning and our End—
you came to us in Jesus Christ
    and you fill everything with your Spirit.
We come because we need you.
We come because we love you as much as we are able.
We come because we choose to trust you to lead us
    on our life journey.
Challenge and correct us.
Heal and encourage us.
Help us believe your welcome
    and accept your call on our lives.

- Teach us.
- Guide us.
- Renew and refresh us.
    May our faithfulness mature in some small way
        during this hour of worship.
- We pray in Jesus' name. Amen.

30 Rain that waters *for Sunday*

Eternal God, you are great and greatly to be praised.
Your word is life and truth.
We have come to hear it.
Like the rain that waters the earth,
    let your Word water our lives.
Let it wash over us like the waves of the sea.
Let it splash our sins away.
Quiet the voices in us and around us
    so that we might hear your voice alone.
Through Jesus Christ our Lord. Amen.

31 A sacred place

(can be used for an ordination to ministry)

Come together in the presence of the eternal God.
    The moment is now.
    The place is here.
In this holy place, may eternity and time overlap.
May this be a sacred place where we know the Lord is our God.
        (moment of silence)
Sovereign God, you call each of us by name.
Give us eyes to see your world around us.
Teach us to hear the voices of your people.
Empower us to cry out for your holy justice.
Strengthen us to love with your unending love.
May we know what we see, rather than see what we know.

May we honor and glorify you,
    and proclaim to future generations what you have
        done for us.
May God's deliverance be proclaimed to a people yet unborn.
Amen.

32 Speak your wisdom

L: God who spoke the world into being,
      speak your wisdom among us today.

P: We seek your wisdom
      to live in shalom with all creation.

L: God who loves the world extravagantly,
      draw us near to your heart this day.

P: We seek to know your perfect love
      that drives out all fear.

L: God who gives bread to the hungry,
      fill us with courage to freely share
      the bread of your Word.

P: We seek your power
      to loosen our shackled tongues
      that the whole world might rejoice to hear
      the Good News of Jesus Christ.

All: Come, let us unite our voices in praise of God!

33 Mother's Day

(based on Psalm 131 and Isaiah 49)

L: El Shaddai, we come humbly before you this day,
      seeking not to walk in ways too difficult for us,
      nor trying to understand things beyond our grasp.

P: Let us quiet ourselves now
      and sit for a moment in God's embrace.

L: Like a satisfied infant at its mother's breast,
      let our souls be tranquil in the embrace of El Shaddai.
   (pause)

L: We sing to you, O God,
      For you have comforted your children.

P: Sing for joy, O heavens, and exult, O earth.
     Break forth, O mountains, into singing!

All: For El Shaddai has compassion
      on the children of her womb.

Praising

34 Life itself

(based on Psalm 23)

Holy Spirit, you are life itself to us.
You refresh our souls,
    just as you green the pastures in springtime.
Your comfort is like a pool of still water.
In your presence, we can face pain and uncertainty.
When we remember you, we are unafraid.
Even our enemies cannot terrify us when you are here.
We are lifted up, along with all things good and merciful.
Throughout our lives, we remain with you.
Thanks be to God! Amen.

35 Creation sings

O Great Composer,
    all creation sings your glory.
Where unity is absent, transform our discord into harmony,
    so that, attuned to you, we may rejoin the mighty chorus
    that sings your praise throughout the world,
    bringing honor to your holy name. Amen.

36 Hallelujah for color

In the hushed quiet of the early dawn,
    when only the starlings and robins
    have found voices to sing,
    we look outside at the awakening world.
You are a God of color, and now we, too, sing.

The crabapple tree is weighed down with glorious pink blooms.
The ornamental pear reaches white-blossomed arms
    high to the heavens;
Tulips of red, orange, purple, pink, white, and yellow
    burst forth in song to greet the morning's light.
And the green—every shade of green—
    is a fugue of grass, bush, flower, and tree.
You are a God of color, and now we, too, sing.

The sky erupts into a choir of indescribable hues.
The gray of dawn is replaced with a symphony
    of faint coral and sparkling lavender.
Patches of brilliant blue peek through billowy white clouds,
    promising a golden day rich in sunshine.
You are a God of color, and now we, too, sing.

May the tune and timbre of our voices
    forever sing out in praise of color;
In praise of God, who planned such a feast
    for our eyes this spring morning.
Hallelujah for color! Amen.

37 Gifts without number

We praise you because you are God
    and because your gifts to us are without number.

We praise you for the breath of life,
 for the beauty of the world,
 and for all that sustains us with bodily strength.
We praise you for a valuable heritage
 that comes to us across many generations of ancestors.
We praise you for work to do
 and for energy to work.
O God, may we never forget to praise you
 for your greatness and your goodness. Amen.

38 Praise the Lord, all you deeps

(based on Psalm 148)

L: Praise the Lord.
P: **Praise the Lord from the heavens.**
 Praise the Lord in the heights!
L: Praise God, all heavenly angels; praise God, all heavenly host!
 Praise God, sun and moon; praise God, all shining stars.
P: **Praise God, you highest heavens**
 and you waters above the heavens!
All: *Let them praise the name of the Lord,*
 for God commanded and they were created.
L: God established them forever and ever;
 God fixed their bounds, which cannot be passed.
P: **Praise the Lord from the earth,**
 you sea monsters and all deeps,
 fire and hail, snow and frost,
 stormy wind fulfilling his command!
L: Mountains and all hills, fruit trees and all cedars,
 wild animals and all cattle,
 creeping things and flying birds!
P: **Rulers of the earth and all peoples,**
 princes and all monarchs of the earth!
 Young men and women alike, old and young together!

All: *Let them praise the name of the Lord,*
      for God's name alone is exalted;
      God's splendor is above the earth and the heavens.

39 Pursue righteousness

(based on Psalm 146)

L: Come let us praise our God.
P: We will praise the Lord as long as we live.
   We will sing praises to our God our whole life long.
L: Do not put your trust in worldly monarchs,
      in whom there is no help.
P: Happy are those whose help is in the God of Jacob
      and the God of Jesus,
L: who made heaven and earth; who keeps faith forever;
P: who brings justice for the oppressed;
      who sets the prisoners free.
L: The Lord will reign forever.
All: *Let us gather together to praise our God!*

40 It is the Lord!

(based on Psalm 30, Revelation 5:11-14, John 21:7)

L: I will exalt the Lord who lifts me
      from the depths of sin and shame!
P: It is the Lord who heals my spirit and body!
L: All you saints, sing your hearts out to God!
   Praise his holy name!
P: It is the Lord who brings rejoicing in the morning
      and turns my wailing into dancing.
L: Join with thousands upon thousands of angels in heaven,
      and every breathing creature on earth,
      in praise to the Lamb who was slain and rose again.

P: **Worthy is the Lamb to receive honor, glory and praise.**
L: It is the Lord!
All: It is the Lord!

41 We are in a blessed place

(based on Psalm 85:8-13)

L: Alleluia. We thank you, Lord, for your great salvation.
All: Blessed Savior, thank you for your goodness and mercy!
L: God's mercy and truth, righteousness and peace—
    they welcome us!
All: We are in a blessed place; blessings abound in our lives!

42 Psalm 119:129-136

(congregational sung Alleluia is HWB 101)

(begin with sung Alleluia)
L: I open my mouth and pant,
    longing for your commands.
  Turn to me and have mercy on me,
    as you always do to those who love your name.
  (sung Alleluia)

L: Direct my footsteps according to your word,
    and let no sin rule over me.
  Redeem me from human oppression,
    that I may obey your precepts.
  (sung Alleluia)

L: Make your face shine upon your servant,
    and teach me your decrees. Amen.

43 Psalm 66:1-9

(congregational sung Alleluia is HWB 101)

L: Make a joyful noise to God all the earth;
      and sing the glory of God's name!
    (sung Alleluia)

L: Give to God glorious praise,
      for the deeds of the Lord are awesome.
    (sung Alleluia)

L: Come and see what God has done.
    Come and let the sound of the Lord's praise be heard.
    (sung Alleluia)

44 Lift us to high places

(based on Psalm 30)

L: We will exalt the one who lifts us to high places.
P: Sing to the Lord, all you saints. Praise God's holy name.
L: We called to you and you healed us.
P: Sing to the Lord, all you saints. Praise God's holy name.
L: Through Jesus, you place our feet on higher ground
P: Sing to the Lord, all you saints. Praise God's holy name.

45 Three-generation praise

Child: I was glad when they said to me,
       "Let us go to the house of the Lord!"
Youth: I was glad when they said to me,
       "Let us go to the house of the Lord!"
Adult: I was glad when they said to me,
       "Let us go to the house of the Lord!"
Child: Standing on holy ground,
Youth: bound firmly together,
Adult: we give thanks to the name of the Lord!

All: *And together we will pray for peace.*
Child: Peace within these walls;
Youth: peace within our family and friends;
Adult: peace within ourselves.
All: *In the house of God, we give thanks*
to the name of the Lord!

46 A testimony of God's power

(based on Psalm 104)

L: Astonishing God, you fill us with awe and amazement.
You are clothed with honor and majesty, wrapped in
light as with a garment. You stretch out the heavens
like a tent; you set the beams of your chamber on the
waters; you make the clouds your chariot; you ride on
the wings of the wind and make of them your messengers.

P: **Your wonderful works are testimony of your kindness,
wisdom, and power. You make the springs gush forth
in the valleys; they flow between the hills giving drink
to every wild animal; the deer quench their thirst. By
the streams the birds of the air have their habitation;
they sing among the branches. How beautiful is your
creation!**

L: You cause the grass to grow for the cattle; you bring
food from the earth and wine to gladden the human
heart. How manifold are your works! In wisdom you
have made them all and the earth is full of your creatures.

P: **These all look to you to feed them in due time; when
you give them food, they gather it up; when you open
your hand, they are filled with good things. When
you hide your face, they are dismayed; when you take
away their breath, they die and return to their dust.**

When you send forth your Spirit, they are created, and you renew the face of the ground.

All: *May the glory of the Lord endure forever; may the Lord rejoice in divine works. I will sing to the Lord as long as I live; I will sing praises to the Lord's name while I have being. May my meditation be pleasing, for I rejoice in the Lord. Alleluia! Amen.*

47 Prayer of praise and thanksgiving

(based on Psalm 33)

Rejoice in the Lord, O you righteous!
Praise befits the upright.
Praise the Lord with the lyre;
    make melody to the Lord with the harp of ten strings.
Sing to God a new song;
    play skillfully on the strings, with loud shouts.
For the word of the Lord is upright,
    and all God's work is done in faithfulness.
God loves righteousness and justice;
    the earth is full of the steadfast love of the Lord!

We do praise you, Lord, for your steadfast love.
We praise you for a night of rest
    and for the gift of another day.
We praise you for opportunities to read and study and learn
    and to be in relationships with people.
We praise you for the great cloud of witnesses
    who have gone before us
    and shaped us and made us who we are.

Our souls wait for you, Lord;
    you are our Help and our Shield.

Our hearts are glad in you
    because we trust in your holy name.
Let your steadfast love be upon us,
    even as we hope in you. Amen.

48 Open our imaginations

Amazing God of mystery and creation,
    root us in love so deep we ride its waves
    and dare to walk with you on water.
Open our eyes and our imaginations
    so that we recognize what is enough
    and dare to offer up what we have for a miracle.
Continue to guide us on this wild journey
    of worship and wonder.
In your holy name we pray. Amen.

49 Artist of awe

Glorious Giver,
    how great is your faith in us,
    to have given us such gifts.
You created us,
    our imaginations,
    and our opportunities.
We praise you, Artist of Awe,
    with every stroke of ink and splash of paint,
    with chiseling of wood and molding of clay,
    with kneading of dough and spooling of thread,
    with the dance of spirit and body,
    with the song of heart and voice.
This is our faith-filled response
    to your redeeming love and your many gifts to us.
All praise to you, now and forever. Amen.

Confessing and Reconciling

50 You call us, and yet . . .

1: Gracious God, we come before you to confess:
we have not lived out the folly of the Gospel.

2: You call us to be poor in spirit,
yet we often place our desires over the needs of
others.

1: You call us to mourn,
yet we insulate ourselves
from the pain surrounding us.

2: You call us to be meek,
yet we struggle to appear strong and superior.

1: You call us to thirst for righteousness,
yet we want to take the easiest path.

2: You call us to be pure in heart,
yet our hearts are pulled in many directions.

1: You call us to be peacemakers,
yet we struggle to live in peace
with those closest to us
and we are too often silent about the warring ways
of our nation.

All: *Forgive us, O God,*
and help us to follow the way of Jesus
ever more faithfully. Amen.

51 Seduced by other gods

Life-giving God, hear our prayer of confession.
We are seduced by the gods of this world.
Materialism coaxes us to trust in things.
Success tempts us to work harder and longer.
Security persuades us to purchase
more and more "protection."
Pride entices us to fall in love with ourselves.
Busyness charms us into believing
there is one more thing we must do.
Perfectionism sweet-talks us into making mountains
out of molehills.
Fear takes captive our creativity and our confidence.
Forgive us for worshipping the gods of this world
who bring only death.
Free us from their grip,
that we might worship you alone. Amen.

52 Failure to accept

In the silence of these moments
we pause to confront ourselves
and name to you the matters
that prevent us from fully realizing your grace.
(pause)
We name things that prevent us from accepting ourselves,
that keep us from accepting one another,
that block us from reaching out
to humankind and to creation.
We abandon ourselves to you in trust;
hear us, love us, and forgive us.
Merciful One, hear our prayer. Amen.

53 We misuse love

(inspired by Matthew 5:43-48 and 1 John 4:7-12, 20-21)

We so easily use and misuse the word *love*.
We say we love our car,
   but we can't stand a co-worker.
We say we love this color of fabric,
   but we snub a brother or sister in Christ.
We make excuses that so-and-so doesn't deserve our love.
Forgive us, gracious God, for not believing or ignoring
   your reconciling love shown in Jesus on the cross.
With you we can love those we cannot love without you.
Through Jesus we pray. Amen.

54 Body of Christ

L: Lord, you have called us the "Body of Christ."
    We confess our yearnings to be one, our hopes of peace—
       but we regret our failings, our lack of unity.
    How can we be Christ's body when we are so flawed?
P: **Help us remember the One who came in human flesh
    and lived among us.**
L: We are the body of Christ?
    How can we make that claim when we are so broken?
P: **Help us remember the broken body of Jesus.**
L: We are the body of Christ?
    How can we say that when we are so sinful?
P: **Help us remember the One who brought forgiveness
    through the cross.**
L: We are the body of Christ?
    How can that be when we are so weak?
P: **Help us remember the One whose Spirit fills us,
    turning weakness to strength.**

L: We are the body of Christ?
How can we make that claim when we are so small?

**P: Help us remember the One whose kingdom comes
as a grain of wheat, feeding the world.**

L: Lord, take us as we are:
human, broken, sinful, weak, and small.

**P: Our hands are your hands.
Our feet are your feet.
Our body is your body.
Equip and send us forth, the body of Christ. Amen.**

55 Fear mixed with hope

All: Holy God, we stand in your presence today.

1: This is a day of new beginnings,

2: a day for trusting your Holy Spirit,

1: a day for considering the wisdom of the ages

2: and the dreams and visions for your new world.

1: We confess that fear is mixed with our hope.

2: Even as we seek together your new work,

1: we find ourselves clinging to the old and familiar.

*All: Embrace us in our hopes and fears,
and set our feet on the path of your new creation. Amen.*

56 We are impatient

(based on Romans 8:12-25)

Hear us, O God; hear our innermost thoughts.

You have declared that the suffering of this world
is nothing compared to the glories of eternal life.

We are not so sure …

We are impatient …

We wonder …

We pray for what we do not yet see and do not yet
understand.

You have promised that through hope we are saved.
It is in hope that we wait.
Hear our prayer, O God. Amen.

57 Forgive our unbelief

(inspired by John 20:19-29 and Psalm 150)

L: Like Thomas, we seek solid proof
      that you are present in our struggles.
P: **Forgive our unbelief.**
L: We collapse in fear and doubt and tremble
      in the face of difficulties.
P: **Forgive our unbelief.**
L: Like the psalmist, give us courage to praise you
      with every breath we take
      and every thing we have!
P: **Praise the Lord. Praise the Lord!**

58 Suspicion, fear and violence

L: Merciful God, we mourn the violence and injustice
      that takes root in many forms
      and in many places far and near.
P: **Merciful God, we thirst for your peace.**
L: We recognize the roots of conflict in ourselves
      and our complicity in systems of power and control.
P: **Merciful God, we thirst for your reconciliation.**
L: We confess that stereotypes, envy, suspicion, and racism
      shape our perceptions and influence our actions.
P: **Merciful God, we thirst for your truth.**
L: We acknowledge that at times we fear our neighbors.
P: **Merciful God, we thirst for your love.**

L: We repent of the ways we contribute
   to suspicion, fear and violence.
   Guide us as we reaffirm our calling as your peacemakers.
   Grant us courage to risk loving each of our neighbors
   at home and around the globe.

All: **Satisfy our thirst by leading us to your living water.**
Amen.

59 Silence and avoidance

(inspired by Isaiah 1:17)

We confess, Lord,
   we have been slow to learn your ways.
We have avoided the orphan and widowed,
   ignored the oppressed,
   and participated knowingly in systems
      that perpetrate injustice.
Our silence in the face of wrong and our denial
   have not made for peace.
Our cowardice has abetted war and violence.
We seek your forgiveness for our failure
   to align ourselves with your purposes
   and with the people for whom you care so deeply.
Lord, be merciful and slow to anger.
Grant us your compassion
   and fill us with the courage of your son, Jesus. Amen.

60 Injustice and unrighteousness

(based on Amos 5:6)

1: God says to us: I know how many are your transgressions,
   and how great are your sins. Seek good and not evil,
   that you may live; and so the Lord will be with you.
   Hate evil and love good, and establish justice in the
   gate; it may be that the Lord will be gracious.

We remember our injustice and unrighteousness.

(silent confession)

2: We have a great high priest who has passed through
the heavens: Jesus, the Son of God. Let us hold fast to
our confession. For he is able to sympathize with our
weaknesses; in every respect has been tested as we
are, yet is without sin. Let us therefore approach the
throne of grace with boldness, so that we may receive
mercy and find grace to help in time of need. Amen.

61 Day and night
(based on Luke 18:8)

L: Day and night we cry out to God for help. We ask for:
1: **food for the hungry,**
2: *power for the powerless,*
All: *justice for the oppressed.*
L: In the middle of the night our hearts cry out,
"God, do something!
1: **"Make things right.**
2: *"Grant us peace.*
All: *"Change the world."*
L: In those moments of darkness, God asks us to participate
in creating a more righteous and peaceful world.
We confess that too often we look for a miracle
when our hands and hearts can be God's means
of granting justice.
(silence)
L: The God who made heaven and earth
helps us to live justly.
All: *Emboldened by God's strength, we remain steadfast*
in our pursuit of what is right and holy and just.

62 Prayer of confession

(sung response is "Oh, Lord have mercy" [STJ 47], stanza 1)

God our Maker, we are your creatures;
    at night we grow weary;
    in the morning we rise with new strength.
God our Savior, we are the ones you rescue
    from aimless wandering and blind despair.
God our Keeper, we are the ones you protect
    from our own good intentions
    and our foolish, self-centered dreams.
We are your children—
    fragile, finite, vulnerable.
    (sung response)

Merciful God,
we fail to love those nearest to us
    with a tender and sturdy love.
We fail to love those on the other side of town
    with generosity and compassion.
We fail to see in our enemies' faces
    your image and your dreams.
Merciful God, we want to see as you see.
    (silence, followed by sung response)

Merciful God,
we waste the gifts of the earth
    and then condemn those whose pantries are bare.
We keep silent when the war goes on
    and we keep investing our wealth in systems that oppress.
We shade the truth
    and speak ill of others when we can get away with it.
Merciful God, we want to be true as you are true.
    (silence, followed by sung response)

And yet, merciful God,
you have made us for yourself.
You long to cleanse us and set us free;
You want to touch our eyes
and open them to the healing truth.
And so, with grateful hearts, we receive your grace.
We are beloved, and in your sight we are made whole. Amen.
(*sung response, repeat twice*)

63 In the wilderness

L: For the ways we have abandoned you
and put ourselves in the wilderness,
P: forgive us, O Lord.
L: For the ways we have marginalized others
and driven them into the wilderness,
P: forgive us, O Lord.
L: For our complaint when, in refining us,
you have led us into the wilderness,
P: forgive us, O Lord.
L: Thank you, O Lord, for being with us in every wilderness.
Amen.

64 We forget to dream

(*based on 1 Kings 8:22-53*)

L: God of all Life,
there is no God like you in all the earth.
You keep your promises and show unfailing love
to all who obey you.
Listen to our prayer, O God,

for even though the highest heavens cannot contain
>   you,
you choose to put your name in this place.
Hear us from heaven and grant us forgiveness.
When we dream dreams that are contrary to your way ...
When we desire what is selfish and short sighted,
>   ignoring our brother's and sister's needs ...
Forgive us.

All: *God have mercy.*

L: When we go on ahead without you ...
When we choose our way, disregarding your spirit's
>   help ...
When we try to fit you in our plans
>   rather than fitting our plans in your will ...
Forgive us.

All: *God have mercy.*

L: When we forget to dream ...
When we accommodate too willingly to "the way
>   things are"
>   and forget to live in your way,
>   working for abundant life for all ...
Forgive us.

All: *God have mercy. Amen.*

Assurance

L: God desires to create in us abundant life, free and full.
God desires to help us fulfill our dreams.
In you, God delights.
May you find your delight in God.

65 Come thou fount

*(based on Psalm 30, Exodus 15, Psalm 143; "Come, thou fount"
[HWB 521] is used as a response)*

We will sing glory to God
　　and will praise and love God forever and forever,
For we cried out from Sheol
　　and God heard our plea and healed us.

It had been three days since we left the Red Sea and began
wandering with Moses through the wilderness. Three
endless days on shifting sand, attempting to navigate in
the glaring sun, walking without water, our feet on fire,
our vision blurred, our souls dry to the bone.

We cried out to the Lord; and to God we made supplication:
　　"What profit is there in death?" we asked.
　　"What is the value of going down into the Pit?"

And then, in the distance, we spied Marah and imagined
the sparkling waters. We dreamed of the restoration of our
bodies, and our spirits sang in the hope that was before us.
　　(congregation sings stanza 1)

But the waters of Marah were bitter. Promises crumbled;
hopes fell away like ashes. God hid his face from us.
　　"Have mercy on us, O God!" we prayed, our souls aching.
　　"Have mercy on us, O God!
　　"Where will we find water?
　　"And what can we give our children to drink?"

Moses turned his back to us. He returned with a piece of
wood and threw it into the bitter water. The water became
sweet, and our weeping turned to joy! Here, in this place,
the Lord established a statute and an ordinance.
　　(congregation sings stanza 2)

Here in this place God put us to the test, saying, "If you listen carefully to the voice of the Lord, and do what is right in God's sight, giving heed to the commandments and statutes, I will heal your diseases and lift up your souls from Sheol."
(congregation sings stanza 3)

Then we came to Elim, where there were twelve springs of water and seventy palm trees. And we camped by the water.
(quiet meditation with one instrumental stanza)

66 Humble before God

1:   Holy God of all life, we humble ourselves before you.
2:   God of justice,
      too many people are weighed down by oppression.
1:   God of freedom,
      too many people are in chains.
2:   God of abundance,
      too many people are hungry.
1:   God of care,
      too many people live in fear.
All: *We cry out to you, Holy God of all life. Answer us.*
      (silence)

Assurance: *Isaiah 58:9-11*

67 Battles within and without

Expansive God, the evil is massive.
The deception is huge.
The noise is shattering.
It is easier to stay in shallow waters,
    to focus on our mass of ailments
    and avoid your larger wooing love.

Come, O Spirit of the living God.
Bring peace to the battles within and without.
Teach us to be still and know
    that you are God. Amen.

68 Requiem for a "deathstyle"

(can be used with Psalm 23 and "Shepherd me, O God" [HWB 519])

1: We've traded the lifestyle Jesus offered
    for the *death*style of empire.
2: We're eating ourselves to death while others starve.
3: The green pastures are full of pesticides
2: and the still waters are unsafe to drink.

1: Many absorb Christian mainstream media—
3: programs full of truth about God's awesome power
    and eternal life in Jesus
2: but laced with lies and the temptations of empire;
1: It's as though death gets all dressed up
    and ready to go shopping
3: for clothes or shoes,
1: or whatever bargain will distract us
2: from the true cost of discipleship.

1: Jesus' message of salvation
2: was a divine invitation
3: to leave the empire-desire behind—
2: to fear no evil,
1: to sit down and eat with our enemies,
3: to anoint one another in service and love.

1: This is the gospel that we are to offer the world:
3: a radical invitation to join the movement
1: where the last are the first
    and the greatest are the least.

2: In the land of gluttony and stylized death,

3: we are peacemakers who share simple meals in
        community.

2: Empowered by the Holy Spirit, we live joyfully.

1: Even here in the valley of the shadow of death,

3: when times are hard and energy low,

2: we lean deeper into the body of Christ the Shepherd
        who cares deeply for this world.

3: Our cups overflow in solidarity
        and a passion for justice.

1: God's goodness and mercy support and lead us.

2: Shepherd us O God,

3: beyond our wants,

1: beyond our fears,

1-3: from death into life!

69 Thinly veiled efforts to have our own way

(based on James 3:18–4:3)

L: Move in our midst, O Spirit of God,
      so our lives will reflect
      the gentleness born of wisdom.

**P: Turn us from envy, boastfulness, and selfish ambition.
Fill us with wisdom from above.**

L: We confess our part in the conflicts and disputes
      among us.

**P: Too often our prayers become thinly veiled efforts
to have our own way.**

L: We need to hear your gentle but firm admonition:

**P: "You ask and do not receive, because you ask wrongly,
in order to spend what you get on your pleasures."**

L: We need to hear your disarming invitation:

**P: "Ask rightly and you will receive grace upon grace,
much more than you could ever imagine!"**

L: Amen.

70 Living in privilege

O God of relentless love,
    ferocious God of peace …
We say we want peace.
We say we are a people of peace.
Yet we entertain violence in our hearts,
    wanting revenge and seeking it.
We live in privilege,
    turning deaf ears to the poor.
O Lamb of God, have mercy on us.

Wrench us from all desires that breed violence.
Fill us with holy anger,
    and make us advocates for those who have no voice.
Spirit of Jesus, come upon us.
Compel us with the fury of your love,
    until the world is flooded with your reconciling hope.
O Lamb of God, grant us peace. Amen.

71 We don't love ourselves enough

Lord, we confess the times
    when we are convinced of being right,
    and when we are afraid to be right.
We mind our own business,
    and neglect what you ask of us.
We refuse to ask for help,
    and we refuse to even try.
We love ourselves too much,
    and we don't love ourselves enough.
We give into our temptations,
    and we claim not to be tempted.
We try to run from you,
    and we try to run from ourselves.

We fail to forgive each other,
   and we fail to forgive ourselves.
Forgive us, we pray. Amen.

72 Working in our own power

L: Holy Spirit, Source of our life,
   hear your children's confession
   and grant us mercy.
   For fearing change
   when you call us to new patterns of living,

P: forgive us.

L: For failing to see your empowering, transforming vision
   for ourselves and for all your creation around us,

P: forgive us.

L: For working out of our own power,
   for dividing rather than uniting
   as we pursue our own agenda rather than yours,

P: forgive us.
   (silence)

***All: We confess that our source of energy, identity, and unity
   is Jesus Christ,***

L: not our political affiliation;
   not our loyalty to sports teams;
   not our wealth or education;
   not our family ties.

All: Christ is our source of energy, identity, and unity.

Assurance

L: Know this: Christ loves you and wants to empower you.
   Christ applauds you like a mother
      applauding her toddler's first steps,
      and will lovingly embrace you when you stumble.
   Walk confidently then,
      through the doors Christ opens for you today.
   Christ is constantly cheering you on. Amen.

73 Where does our help come from?

(based on Psalm 121)

Lord, we lift up our eyes,
> to our government and to our stock market.*
Is that where our help comes from?

No, our help comes from you, O Lord.
You made heaven—and this earth,
> where governments and economic institutions* are built.
You stand ready to bail us out,
> even when we run to politicians
> and our financial investments.

We so readily look to this world
> when we're sick or unemployed or retired.
But you have ensured the well-being of your people
> for generations
> and will continue to do so beyond our days on earth.
Forgive us our misplaced quests for help. Amen.

Assurance
Brothers and sisters,
> the God of our Lord Jesus Christ is faithful
> and has shown us perfect love through our Lord Jesus.
By the power of the Holy Spirit,
> let us now share Christ's peace.
Let us live as a people set free from the fear of this world.

* Adapt to substitute Washington, D.C. or Ottawa, Wall Street or Bay Street.

74 Status over service

God of salvation:
When our works fail to meet the promise of our words,
    show us.
When we value status over service, humble us.
When we burden others
    through false dependence or independence, forgive us.
When we come penitent before you, have mercy upon us.
When we speak with muted voices, hear our hearts.
In the name of Christ our Redeemer, we pray. Amen.

75 Disarm our hearts

God of mercy and grace:
We mourn the lives of those around the world
    who are daily affected by terrorism and violence.
We acknowledge that violence is a web that traps us all.
We confess our own complicity
    when our own government feeds terrorism and violence
    to protect our interests and lifestyles.
Forgive us our thoughts and acts
    that dehumanize those we consider enemies.
We look into our own hearts and confess our own desires
    for vengeance and retaliation
    against those who have harmed us.
Forgive us our violence
    as we forgive those who commit violence against us.
Disarm our hearts as well as our hands
    through the transforming power of the Spirit of Jesus.
    Amen.

Praying

Prayers of Healing

76 Healed and still healing

God our Healer,
>you have already healed us in many ways—
>and still we know our need for healing.

We thank you for the healing we have received:
>for relationships, now mended by your healing touch,
>for bodies racked with pain, now made free,
>for emotions once crippling us, finally restored by
>>love.

At the same time, we come to you for healing—
>for wounds that have injured our spirits
>>and continue to stab us,
>for words said to us, perhaps even unknowingly,
>>that have killed our joy,
>for actions against us and those we love,
>>that have nearly crushed our breath from us.

For all this and much more—we need your healing touch.
Amen.

77 Hectic lives

(based on Matthew 14:13-21)

Shepherd God, when our lives become hectic,
    lead us away to a peaceful place.
Smile on us with compassion,
    heal our sickness, and restore those we love.
Keep us close to you, and provide what we need.
Fill us with your blessings, and send us out
    to share your compassion with the world. Amen.

78 A physician's prayer

Great Physician and Healer,
    we come to you with heavy hearts and weary minds.
Our lives are fragile. Our bodies are mortal.
In illness, we feel broken, betrayed, and battered.
The demands of our lives take a heavy toll.
How can it be, we wonder,
    that you allow such pain and brokenness?

And then we remember the cross.
You too were broken.
You too were betrayed.
And yes, indeed, you were battered.

It is through your suffering that humanity finds healing.
In your broken bones we receive fresh strength.
In your lacerated flesh we draw new life.
In your wounded spirit we are made whole.

May your presence be known in the midst of our brokenness.
We pray for healing that transcends medicine,
    hope that can only be ascribed to you,
    and wholeness beyond human measure. Amen.

79 Our frailty

Gentle God, in our limitations and uncertainties,
    we acknowledge our frailty.
We are vulnerable like small children in need of care.
We call out to you as a baby cries for the care of a mother.
You remind us that we must be like children
    to enter your kingdom.
And so, mothering God, we offer ourselves to you,
    fragile and vulnerable.
Pick us up and rock us in your arms,
    nurse us with your spirit,
    and heal us with your tender care. Amen.

80 A prayer for our hearts

Gracious God, you welcome us with a gentle heart.
We come to you with aching and divided hearts
    broken by imperfect relationships.
Heal our hearts, Lord, heal our hurts.
Help us let go of selfish desires
    that destroy relationships.
Release us from our desperate need for security.
Free us from the guilt that binds us.
Mold our hearts with sensitivity and compassion—
    love for our neighbors near and far,
    grace for our families and our churches,
    thankfulness for your daily blessings,
    and clarity to focus on your true kingdom treasures.
In the name of Jesus,
    who loves us with a Shepherd's heart. Amen.

Prayers of Illumination

81 Pre-sermon

We ask for ears to hear your word,
    eyes to see your Spirit,
    hearts to feel your life,
    wisdom to receive your words, your Spirit, your life.
Amen.

82 Lift us up

(based on John 3:14)

Faithful God . . .
Lift our eyes from present distress to your promised presence.
Lift our hearts from anxious thought
    to the quiet confidence of a child with its mother.
Lift our hands from binding work into the freedom of praise.
Lift our lives from our feverish pace
    into a gentler rhythm of service.
Failing this, O God,
    we will not see the one they lifted up in scorn,
    the one you lift up in love for us. Amen.

83 Approved by God

(can follow a reading of 2 Timothy 2:15)

You approve of us.
You look at our bodies-
    our 23- and 53- and 73-year-old bodies,
    and you say, "It is good."
You see our minds renewed in baptism,

our dreams and reflections,
and you declare, "It is good."
You see our future, unrealized in our present
and unknown to our imagination,
and you insist, "It is good."
Thus approved,
we present ourselves to you as mirrors of your life,
as projections of your light,
as heartbeats of your love—
to assert the truth in a world accustomed to lies,
to measure our words in a world of bombastic speech,
to craft dignity in a world that dismantles it,
to sculpt hope in a world of despair,
to paint peace in a world at war.
May your kingdom come (soon!)
and your will be done (fully!)
on earth as it already is in heaven
and ever shall be! Amen.

84 Abide in us

(can follow readings of John 15:1-15 and Revelation 22:1-21)

Abide in our intellect, that we may think of you.
Abide in our intuition, that we may delight in your glory.
Abide in our speech, that we may honor you.
Abide in our decisions, that we may be just and merciful.
Abide in our actions, that we may participate in your mission
among and beyond us. Amen.

85 Tend our spirits

(after reading Philippians 4:10-14)

Tend to our bitterness of spirit, mighty and merciful One.
Save us from hurts too long unforgiven
and sufferings too deeply cherished.

Save us from cynicism too quickly felt
and revenge too often sought.
Save us from loyalty too easily spurned
and hope too soon abandoned.

Surprise us with your transformation.
In all the places we gasp for air,
breathe your sweet fresh Spirit.
In all the places we see few options,
burst our tired old categories
with your endlessly inventive possibilities.
In all the places we are so sure everything has died,
infuse your unfailing, irrepressible life.

Neither be content with us as we are
nor let us be content as we are.
Instead, push us, pull us,
into new worlds of your making. Amen.

86 Choose life

(based on Psalm 1)

L: Blessed are the faithful ones
who seek the path of integrity.
1: The faithful are like fountains
that spray and dance in sunlight.
2: The faithful shower joy and delight
upon their communities.

L: The evil ones in the world are not so.
1: Their thoughtless actions destroy
a wholesome environment.
2: Their misuse of power leads only to death
and destruction.
All: God of righteousness, help us choose life and not death.

L: Because every secret thought shapes how we live
and every concrete action sculpts who we are,
our choices matter.

All: *While we have the gift of breath, we want to choose life.*
God of righteousness, grant us wisdom to walk in
your ways.

87 Prayer for our thorns

(can follow a reading of 2 Corinthians 12:1-10)

Today, O God, we boldly ask you to de-thorn us.
Remove the dissatisfaction with our work;
    polish the dullness of intellect;
    revive the tired body;
    fix the wounded emotion that has never quite healed;
    yank the secret thorn we fear to name but know too well.
Take these thorns away.

Yet you may refuse—
        not because you are mean or angry
        but because you know, even if we do not,
    that the particular thorn embedded in us
     is even now becoming the means of our wholeness,
    made possible by your power amid our weakness.

Therefore we do not boast of our many successes—
        our grade point average,
        our professional standing in our community,
        our stellar annual evaluation,
        our growing congregation,
        our fine new building addition,
        our children's accomplishments.
No! We boast of our thorns—or rather, of you in the thorns.
It is you who makes us what we are and not we ourselves.
We pray these things in faith and hope. Amen.

88 A refugee's claim

(based on Psalm 2)

Ever-watchful One, you guard and protect me,
    so who will make me afraid?
You feed and clothe me,
    so whom shall I fear?
Although officials hound me and force me underground,
    I do not despair.
They threaten to deport me,
    but I remain confident.
Daily I pray for a good job and a life without fear.
I dream of stretching out my arms in sunlight
    and crossing a border in freedom.
One day I will present a thank offering to you
    and celebrate with my guitar.

Ever-present One, hear me when I cry to you.
Answer me soon. Do not delay!
My family has been tortured and killed.
My country labels me a traitor.
You are my only support.
I wait for you.
Do not turn your back on me. Amen.

89 Direct our eyes

(can follow a reading of 1 Samuel 16:1-13)

Often we do not see as you do.
You see leadership in David,
    the youngest and most rustic of eight sons,
    looking deeper than the handsome head of curly hair,
    the photogenic square-set jaw,
    the smile of straight white teeth.

In David we watch you look perceptively
    into the youngest, the least, the last.
You see possibilities that we, in our ordinariness,
    glance over as inconsequential.

Direct our eyes away from the glamorous glitter,
    the sheen of polished commercials,
    the luster of surface appearance.
Let us see your Good Friday and Easter Jesus—
    the One whom Caesar Augustus,
    mighty ruler of the world's superpower, did not see.
Let us see the One whom important people in the empire
    regarded as an insignificant bug
    to squash between their jeweled fingers.
Let us see the One who died on a cross—
    not some pretty piece of gold-plated metal
    to wear around one's neck,
    but an instrument of state torture and humiliation.
Direct our eyes to that Jesus—
    the One who had no form or beauty that we would
        want to see.

With him in our eyes, let us perceive
    the most creative, the most daring, the most loving,
    the most wildly imaginative thing ever done.
With him in our eyes, let us not be merely impressed—
    let us be dazzled. Amen.

90 Careless prayers

Sometimes we pray carelessly for transformation.
But at this moment we pray differently.
We suspect how uncomfortable, how painful, how pricey,
    our transformations might be.

Will you knock over one of the pillars
    that holds up the house of our belief?
Will you slip in uninvited,
    and snatch away the security blanket
    that no longer comforts us?
Will you back us into some corner
    and with a determined gleam in your eye,
    inform us that what we thought was just and right
    is in fact not?
Will you put a belt around our waist
    and take us where we do not want to go?
What price will we pay for transformation?
What does prayer cost?

Yet if in wisdom you choose to transform us,
    however reluctant we may be,
    however much we may kick and scream and claw,
    then we do ask for life.
We ask for your life—
    life that shepherds us beyond our hopes,
    beyond our fears,
    beyond the final frontier of death itself.
If you push us into a world of alternate possibility,
    then please hold our hand and go with us.

So bless us, not because we deserve it,
    but because you love us. Amen.

91 Revolutionary

(based on Psalm 126)

Revolutionary Energy, you topple regimes and dictators
    and leave others tottering on the brink of destruction.
Shackled nations tremble
    as they glimpse the miracles you birth.

The dispirited begin to hum.
We smile and open our lips in song.
A new re-creation is occurring!
We celebrate your energy within us,
      which revolutionizes all our days. Amen.

Prayers of Intercession

92 Light for others

Creator of Light, thank you for gathering us
      to this place of worship in the light of this day.
Scatter the darkness from our hearts and minds.
May your light comfort the hearts and minds
      of all who grieve this day ...
      (supply specifics from context)
May your light heal the minds and bodies
      of all who struggle with illness ...
      (supply specifics from context)
May your light illumine the hearts and minds
      of all who serve devotedly in the name of Christ....
      (supply specifics from context)
Send forth your light of healing and peace
      into all the world, we pray,
      in the name of Jesus, the light of the world. Amen.

93 Prayer for the world

O God, patient mother of us mortals,
    hear our prayer for the whole human race.
We pray for ourselves and for everyone
    who is separated from you by sin; draw us to Christ.
    (silence and/or free prayers)
We pray for the church in every place,
    for its unity and mission; make it a sign of your reign.
    (silence and/or free prayers)
We pray for those who hold positions of public trust;
    make them just and merciful.
    (silence and/or free prayers)
We pray for those who long to love and be loved,
    for those in faithful relationships and those estranged;
    let love cast out fear.
    (silence and/or free prayers)
We pray for peace
    and for a just sharing of the earth's resources;
    help us see our neighbor's good as our own.
    (silence and/or free prayers)
This we ask in the strong name of Jesus Christ. Amen.

94 Fragments made whole

God who deeply feels our joys and pains
    as if they were your own,
    in you our pleasures find meaning,
    in you our brokenness is made whole.
We pray for our congregation, [*name*],
    that we may become witnesses
    to your reign of peace and reconciliation.

We pray for all people of faith—
    for our fellow Christians
    and for our sisters and brothers of other religions,
    that we may hold on to the revelation we have been given,
    and share it boldly and humbly
    with those seeking a spiritual home.
We pray for the world that you love,
    this world that Jesus longs to embrace.
For warring nations, we pray for peace.
For those who are impoverished,
    we pray for the gift of enough.
For those who are affluent,
    we pray for the gift of generosity.
For those in positions of leadership,
    we pray for wisdom and attentiveness to justice.
All these fragments we offer to you,
    the One who gathers us all and makes us whole. Amen.

95 According to your will

How should we pray at a time like this? I will read a prayer — and pause to give you a moment to pray silently. We'll end with the Lord's prayer.

All: ***Gracious God, send us your Holy Spirit***
       so we might pray according to your will.

L: We pray for the church in every place
       and for the ministry Christ has given each of us.
       (silence and/or free prayers)

L: We pray for the peace of the world,
       that respect and forbearance might grow,
       that oppression and vengeance might be overcome.
       (silence and/or free prayers)

L: We pray for those in positions of public trust,
       that they might serve justice and promote freedom.
       (silence and/or free prayers)

L: We pray for blessing on all human labor,
       that the riches of creation might be used
       for the common good.
       (silence and/or free prayers)

L: We pray for those in poverty, danger, and suffering,
that they might be set free and given hope.
(silence and/or free prayers)

L: We pray for those who make us their enemies.
We pray for ourselves when we become the enemy.
May we find forgiveness and be transformed.
(silence and/or free prayers)

L: We thank you for the bounty of nature,
the treasures of culture, meaningful work,
and the bonds of human community.
Most of all we thank you for your immeasurable love
in the redemption of the world
through our Lord Jesus Christ.
(silence and/or free prayers)

L: Now we pray as Jesus taught us, saying, Our Father ...

96 For HIV/AIDS victims

(best prayed in unison and adapted from its African context)

In this season of great danger among our people,
we agree that our calling as followers of Jesus
urges us to choose life not only for ourselves,
but also for our neighbors.
Therefore, as a matter of conscience,
we give our sacred word to one another and to God,
that, honoring each other, we will care tenderly
for those who suffer and those who grieve.
We will defend those who are vulnerable to abuse.
We will hold ourselves to the highest personal standard
of sexual conduct:
abstinence before and faithfulness in marriage.
We will know our own status,
and will not endanger others or ourselves.
We will prepare the young
to face the present perils successfully
and go on to live full and joyous lives of grace and faith.
God help us in this high endeavor, for Jesus' sake. Amen.

97 A prayer in response to 9/11

(can be used in context of violence and loss of life)

God of all comfort, we confess our bewilderment,
    our sadness, anger, and fear.
Hear our prayers.
Surround those who mourn the loss of loved ones.
Embrace them with your loving arms.
Comfort those who long for the missing.
Carry them in your loving arms.
Protect those who risk their lives in rescue efforts.
Strengthen them with your loving arms.
Remind us that your love is stronger than hate.
Keep us from becoming the evil we deplore.
Give us wisdom and restraint.
With trembling faith we pray, O God,
    for a sure sense of your presence in our grieving.
Embrace us with your loving arms.
In you alone do we trust. Amen.

98 After a disaster

Merciful God, the pain of this day is beyond comprehension.
People's homes are lost and family members are dead
    because of this terrible disaster.
In our sorrow, in our fear, yes, even in our anger,
    we look to you for comfort and solace,
    the Creator of heaven and earth.
Comfort, O comfort your people!
Join our cries to the groans of creation
    that all will be made whole in you.
(prayer for people who have lost property or loved ones.)

In this dark time, we remember that you walk with us
and wrap your comforting arms around us.
Go with us as we begin the work of picking up the pieces.
Grant us the strength found in your community.
We pray in the name of our Lord and Savior, Jesus Christ.
Amen.

99 For a church closing

L: We have assembled to worship,
just as our founding fathers and mothers did years ago.
P: Let us rejoice in the steadfast love and grace of God.
L: We have inherited many gifts through the efforts
of those who went before us.
P: Let us thank God for the good foundation they laid.
L: As we have done for years,
we gather together on this final day.
**P: We trust God has heard all the prayers
uttered in this place.**
L: We confess our mixed feelings, both gratitude and grief.
P: We open our hearts to the Lord.
L: As we close the church and depart from this place today,
may we go in anticipation of what God has in store
for this building, and for us.
P: We give thanks to the Lord.

100 For an institutional crisis

Healing God, we pray for healing and comfort;
for your light to shine in our pain, confusion and anger.
May everyone touched by this crisis
be sustained by your love in a deep and abiding way.
We ask for strength and wisdom
for those making decisions about the future.

We pray that your people will respond
    graciously and without judgment.
May your Spirit blow fresh winds
    of healing, hope, comfort, and light.
Jesus Christ, light of the world,
    do not let our darkness conquer us.
Let your love embrace and heal us.
We entrust this situation to your care
    believing that you will give us a future and a hope.
    Amen.

Prayers of Petition

101 Christ be our light

L: In the darkness of uncertainty,
    when we don't know what to do,
    when decisions are hard to make,
    light up our darkness.
All: *Christ be our light.*
L: In the darkness of our anxiety
    when we are worried about the future,
    when we don't know where to turn,
    light up our darkness.
All: *Christ be our light.*
L: In the darkness of our despair,
    when life seems empty,
    when we feel there is no future worth seeking,
    light up our darkness.
All: *Christ be our light.*
L: Lord Jesus, you are the light of the world;
    where there is oppression, injustice, and poverty,
    light up our darkness.
All: *Christ be our light. Amen.*

102 A prayer for the wildly successful

(associated with Philippians 3:7-11)

You are great and wondrous, O Christ.
You are able to change the lives of all people.
Instead of praying only for the transformation of people
    who have made a mess of their lives,
    we pray today for the transformation of those
    who are wildly successful in the world's eyes:
We pray for the children who are admitted into gifted programs
      because of their unusual intelligence;
    the students who receive a merit scholarship
      for outstanding academic accomplishments;
    the *summa cum laude* and *magna cum laude* graduates;
    the teachers voted most outstanding in the school;
    the workers who win the employee of the year award;
    the business owners who earn more profit this year
      than in any other.
    (substitute others relevant to your congregation)
At the right time,
    astound each one with your risen, irresistible glory;
    convince them, as you convinced Paul,
    that all their successes, though wonderful,
    are rubbish when compared to knowing you. Amen.

103 May we do your will

Transforming God,
    we beg for softer, gentler,
    less fearful, more gracious and generous hearts.
Protect us from our need to control.
Make us more humble, loving, and poor in spirit.
Lead us into new paths of peace.
We pray, too, for the transformation of our world.

May the nations, leaders, and peoples of this planet
    turn and embrace your way of humility, poverty, charity.
Empower us to name the lies
    and oppose the seductive powers of dominion in our day.
Rebuild your church.
Raise up a whole new generation
    of saints willing to let go of all distractions
    and willing to take risks for your kingdom.
In poverty, humility, and charity
    we pray with Francis of Assisi ...
Enlighten our darkness, and give us
    correct faith and trust,
    firm hope,
    perfect love (even for our enemies)
    wisdom and perception,
    that we may do what is truly your most holy will. Amen.

104 Teach us to find you, the Center

L: Centering God,
        who through Christ, holds all things together,
        we confess we often feel
        we are spinning out of control,
        pulled into somebody else's plans,
        pressed into work we didn't expect,
        propelled into countless places of need.
    Jesus, walk with us in the flurry of our lives.
    Teach us how to find you, the Center.
All: *Teach us how to find you, the Center.*

L: Creating God,
        who through Christ, brings unlikely things together,
        we confess we often feel bombarded,
        with way too much information,
        bewildered by the amount of good things to care for,

    intimidated by the pace of new technology,
        unnerved by how to choose among all the choices.
    Jesus, walk with us in the choices of our lives.
    Teach us how to find you, the Center.
All: **Teach us how to find you, the Center.**

L: Surprising God,
        who calls all things together through Christ,
        we believe you are constantly summoning us
            to pay attention,
        calling us to set aside our agenda and listen,
        beckoning us to set aside our priorities and pray,
        urging us to set aside our itinerary and follow.
    Jesus, walk with us as we learn to live faithfully in the
        world.
    Teach us how to find you, the Center.
All: **Teach us how to find you, the Center. Amen.**

105 Prayer for peace

God, our Maker,
    your love transcends political borders,
        economic barriers, and social classes.
It reaches across the world to all peoples everywhere.
Thank you for your gracious Spirit that moves among us.

God, our Reconciler,
        you yearn for peace and hold before us
        the vision of a peaceable kingdom—
        "on earth as it is in heaven."
Forgive our silence,
        our complacency,
        our prejudice,
        our complicity.
    Forgive us for blurring your vision or discarding our hope.
    Forgive us for not loving our enemy.

God, our shalom,
> we entrust each peacemaker to you.

Empower us all to speak boldly, act justly, and love mercy
> as we walk with you in an increasingly militarized world.

May our congregations and communities reflect your light.

May they be beacons of a radical love that invites,
> encourages,
> reconciles,
> building peace across the world.

In the name of God our Creator, Christ our Peacemaker,
> and the Holy Spirit, our constant Companion. Amen.

106 Irritating logs

(based on Matthew 7:1-5 and Luke 6:27-31)

1: I don't get them, God.
How can they be such jerks and treat me like this?
I'm nice to them!

2: *Are you sure?*

1: Well, they're so arrogant
> they think they're right and everyone else is wrong!

2: *And you're right about this?*
Do you by any chance think they're stupid?

1: Oh.

2: *Wellll …*

1: They're just mean! They call us names
> and say horrible things about me and my friends!

2: *Hmmm …*
(long pause)

2: *Welllllll…..*

1: All right!
So how do I get this irritating log out of my eye?

2: *I thought you'd never ask!*
Try starting with Jesus' words. He gets it.
"Love your enemies.

"Do good to those who hate you.
"Bless those who curse you.
"Pray for those who abuse you.
"Do to others as you would have them do to you."

107 I will be still and learn of you

L: In our lives full of noise and motion,
busyness, activity and pressure,
we want to stop.
We want to clear a place for you, O God.

P: I will be still and learn of you, Spirit of Life within.

L: A great gulf exists between our two lives:
our outer life of work, roles, and responsibility,
dependent on external conditions
and the perceptions of others,
and our inner life where our spirits
are enriched by God's gracious presence.

P: I will be still and learn of you, Spirit of Life within.

L: We long for times of refreshment away from pollution:
noise pollutants of engines, gadgets, gossip;
sight pollutants of billboard, litter, pornography;
spirit pollutants of prejudice, pessimism, put-downs.

P: I will be still and learn of you, Spirit of Life within.

L: We seek release from oppressive feelings that bind us:
fear, resentment, anxiety, regret, and guilt.
Put within us peace, a forgiving spirit,
true repentance, and great faith.

P: I will be still and learn of you, Spirit of Life within.

L: We clear a place for you, O God,
because we hear of your greatness,
we see your grace in our lives,
and we desire to live fully aware in your presence.

P: We will be faithful in waiting for you. Amen.

108 Deep root

May Jesus' life take deep root in us,
    so that today we will respond rather than react,
        understand rather than judge,
        care rather than criticize,
    so that we will seek the good of those who would harm us;
    and trust in you instead of our own defenses. Amen.

109 Bless our enemies

God of all people and nations,
    we don't know how to act when what we love is
        threatened,
    when our beautiful, fragile diverse world
    is in danger of being destroyed.
We want justice! Justice now!
We wish you would forget mercy for awhile, God,
    until you help us get this mess cleaned up ...
But then we realize that we too are complicit
    in things that harm your hopes for us—
    and mercy suddenly looks a lot better.
May we realize that in your cosmic economy
    there is no "other" at all;
    there is only "us."
Bless our enemies;
    in their genuine well-being we all find well-being.
We pray in Jesus' name. Amen.

110 Tightly clenched fists

Provider and Sustainer,
    we are tempted to hold on to everything you give us.

We clench our fists
    because we fear there won't be enough—
    for ourselves or our children—
    if we let go.
Teach us to trust you
    to open our hands and give away
    what you have placed within our reach.
May we share your goodness and blessing
    so that others might see your love.
For surely it is more blessed to give than to receive. Amen.

Prayers and the Trinity

111 God's story with humanity

Holy and most merciful God:
You are our light and our salvation.
You created humanity from the humble dust of the earth.
You delivered those enslaved in Egypt
    and made them into the people of Israel.
Through the prophets and the priests,
    you guided them with wisdom and compassion.
You forgave their violence and their misdeeds
    and never ceased to love them.
And in due time, you sent us Jesus the Messiah.
Jesus declared the reign of God
    and taught us about love, humility, and justice.
Jesus was crucified by the world,
    but you raised him from the dead.
You sent the Holy Spirit to be our everlasting Guide
    in the way of peace,
        to bring us out of enslavement and violence
        and into your righteous reign.

This is the story in which we find ourselves, O God.
In the midst of death, oppression, deceit,
    uncertainty, sorrow, and anguish,
    we live and trust in your Holy Spirit.
We remember this story and look forward
    to the coming fulfillment of your reign.
All praise to the God of our Lord Jesus Christ
    now and forevermore. Alleluia and Amen.

112 Divine Trinity

O divine Wisdom, we trust in you.
O divine Love, we rest in you.
O divine Joy, we delight in you.
May we hear your call to be your church for your people
    that we might become wise, loving, and joyful peacemakers
    through your power. Amen.

113 Holy thanksgiving

Holy, holy, holy, great God of hosts!
The earth is full of your glory!
May we hear your call.
May we know the assurance of your love,
    the equipping ministry of your Spirit,
    and your ever-present guidance and care.
You call each of us into your ministry of reconciliation,
    into the body whose head is Christ,
    a church family that stretches from coast to coast
    and around the world.
Your love affirms our small efforts, forgives our sins,
    and shepherds us beside still waters.
Your Spirit equips and resources the church
    and enables gifts to emerge and blossom.

Your continued guidance affirms risk-taking,
    creative action, and proactive initiative
        that sends us with your gospel message.
Lead, challenge, and bless us.
May our worship—and our sending—be a collective voice
    of thanksgiving and praise to you, our holy Lord. Amen.

114 Three-in-one

Holy God, in creation you shaped us in your image
    and breathed into us the breath of life.
In our sinfulness, you send your Son to show us
    how to live in redemption and grace.
By your Spirit you provide us
    with varieties of gifts for service
    and promptings to use them.
We worship you, Creator, Redeemer and Sustainer.
Send us forth, redeemed and equipped,
    so we may attest to your glory,
    God the Creator,
    Christ the Redeemer,
    Holy Spirit, our Sustainer,
    three in One. Amen.

Communion prayers and invitations

115 Confession in preparation for Communion

Healing God:
You invite us to open our hearts and lives
    to your cleansing presence.

You promise that whatever is fragile or weak or broken
    can be restored in your gracious love.
Touch us tenderly as we wait in silence.
(a time of silence)

Refresh our souls
    with your abundant mercy,
    and feed us with your grace.
Make us ministers of peace to one another,
    in your church, and in all the world.
We pray in the name of Jesus, Prince of Peace,
    who heals and redeems us all. Amen.

116 At the table

L: God of all people,
      at the table of remembrance
      we receive the bread from a brother or sister and
        we say:
All: *Amen. Let your will be done in us.*

L: Nourish us with the body of Christ,
      so that our bodies are fit for service,
      for proclamation,
      for suffering,
      for unity in the Spirit.
    Light of the world,
      at the table of discipleship
      we receive a cup from a brother or sister and we say:
All: *Amen. Let your will be done in us.*

L: Fill us so the blood of Christ
      renews our faith,
      sustains our community,
      cleanses our conscience,
      and directs our energy.

Until we feast at the final resurrection,
>let us here taste and see that the Lord is good.
We thank you for these gifts
>prepared for us before the foundations of the world.
Amen.

117 Bread of life and fruitful Vine

L: Bread of life and fruitful Vine,
P: **you feed our bodies with the gifts of earth;**
you delight our souls with abundant grace;
you nourish our spirits with eternal love.
L: As we receive your life,
P: **strengthen our desire for your presence;**
deepen our trust in your goodness;
renew our hope in your gracious reign.
All: *For you are the Source of our life,*
and we depend upon your mercy. Amen.

118 Prayer before Communion

Jesus, on our journey
>the road is often long and hard and lonely.
Forgive us our blindness,
>our desire to turn back,
>our lack of faith.

We come to meet you today at this table.
Open our eyes to your presence in our lives.
Empower us to truly walk as your children.
Thank you for this feast of love,
>full of mystery and yet full of tangible gifts—
>the gifts of bread and cup and community.
Fill us with your Spirit and give us courage.

We remember now your life, death, and resurrection,
    as we pray the prayer you taught us to pray:
Our Father . . .

119 *Didache**

Words of institution for the bread: 1 Corinthians 11:23-24

Prayer of thanks for the bread
We give you thanks, O Divine Nourishment,
    for the bread of life made known to us
    through your servant Jesus.
To you be the glory forever. Amen.

Words of institution for the cup: 1 Corinthians 11:25-26

Prayer of thanks for the cup
We give you thanks, O Divine Refreshment,
    for the holy vine made known to us
    through your servant Jesus.
To you be the glory forever. Amen.

Closing prayer
As this broken loaf was scattered upon the hills as grain,
    and was gathered together and made one,
    so let your church be gathered together
    into your kingdom from the ends of the earth.
For yours is the glory and the power
    through Christ Jesus forever. Amen.

120 Communion invitation

1:   Come, you who hunger,
        filled with wanting and waiting.

* The title of the second century document from which these prayers are taken. Among other things, the *Didache* outlines early church practices of communion.

2: Come, you who thirst
for the peace of Christ.
All: *Come to the table of the Lord.*
1: Come, not because you are worthy
to sit at Christ's table.
2: Come because you are willing
to serve at Christ's side.
All: *Come to the table of the Lord.*
1: For the Lord our God has gathered us here
and Jesus the Christ is our Host.
2: Come, you who are blessed;
Come, you who are broken.
All: *Come to the table of the Lord.*

121 Inclusive invitation to the communion table

(when children, youth, and unbaptized adults come to the table with the baptized*)

Friends, our dance with God begins in mystery
as God knits each of us in our mother's womb.
Through the mists of time, God loves us
and continues to reach out to us
wherever we are on the journey of faith.
Jesus still welcomes and blesses us all, including children,
with all our wonder and all our questions;
at all our stages of faith.

So to all of you who love God, but are not baptized
or cannot renew your baptismal vows today—
come and receive the blessings of our Lord's table.
Know that God loves you, welcomes your love,
and is with you here.
Know that this church, a part of the body of Christ,
welcomes you, loves you, and needs you.

* Some congregations offer a blessing; others offer grapes or crackers
to children, youth, and others not taking the bread or the cup.

And to all of you who have entered the covenant of baptism,
    who have freely chosen Jesus and his church
    as the center of your lives,
    come, remember, and renew your covenant.
Eat the bread and drink the wine of the new covenant.
Allow the Holy Spirit to reveal the many joyful signs
    of God's reign among us.
May God lead you into ever greater participation
    in that gracious realm.
Come and partake of this feast with thankful hearts.

Miscellaneous Prayers

122 For congregational sharing

God, hear all that we share.
Christ, hold all that we share.
Spirit, move through all that we share. Amen.

123 For governance
(can be used in interfaith public settings)

O Divine Spirit:
We are aware of your greatness
    in the vast turning of the earth toward the sun,
    in the love of our friends and families,
    in the capabilities granted our leaders
    for good and faithful governance.

May what is enacted here today witness
    to the divine intention and hope for human destiny.
May each one of us understand ourselves as beloved.

May we care for allies, opponents, constituents,
    activists, interests, and friends—
      for all are a valued and beloved loved part
    of your divine house, your divine economy.

May those who serve in this institution,
    be actors and instruments of a greater grace,
    a greater hope,
    a greater work that will rise above
      the ordinary run of fear and greed.
May they be made worthy of the divine intention and hope
    for this human community.
May freedom be served and may justice be done.
Above all, may we be governed by a powerful love—
    our true birthright and destiny.
May it be so. Amen.

124 Something new

(can be used in interfaith public settings)

Spirit of life, today we seek something new.
We long for a fresh perspective, an unusual viewpoint,
    a re-framed perception of the problems before us.
We want a fresh take on our opportunities,
    a new look at things for which we hope.
We seek something that sparks the brains' pathways,
    loosens the bones, and quickens the breath.

Today, we seek the original, the exceptional.
May there be non sequiturs and surprises
May there be much good humor.
May fun find its place beside commitment,
    increasing our joy as we set our hearts and minds
    to these our daily tasks, our daily dose of labor.

May we be surprised by some new fairness.
May justice spring forth.
May there be conciliation in our relationships
    and healing in our bodies.
May there be a new and strong hope for each one gathered
    here.
May things be fresh today.
May there be the good that is beyond all our expectations,
    O Spirit of Hope, in whom all things are made new. Amen.

125 Living examples of conviction

(can be used on Heritage Sunday)

God of the ages, we are thankful for our heritage.
You created us in your image and sent us your Son.
Our forefathers and mothers chose to follow you in life.
Many saints preserved the faith by living their convictions.
Our parents and the church shepherded us in the faith.
Grant us the pledge of loyalty to the faith entrusted us
    so that with the saints, we can join around the throne
    and sing your praises through Jesus Christ our Lord. Amen.

Responding

126 Take up the cross

L: Take up the cross and journey with Jesus;
P: happy are those who walk in the ways of the Lord.
L: Take up the cross and follow Christ's teachings;
P: happy are those who delight in the law of the Lord.
L: Take up the cross and become a disciple;
P: happy are those who choose righteousness.
L: Take up the cross and celebrate life;
P: happy are those whose hearts are refreshed by Christ.

127 We proclaim Christ

(based on Colossians 1:15-28)

L: It is Christ whom we proclaim—
P: the image of God;
       the firstborn of all creation;
       the head of the church;
       the beginning and the end;
       the reconciler of all things;
       the peacemaker of the cross;
       the hope and mystery of glory.
L: It is Christ whom we proclaim!

128 Children's affirmation of faith

(people's part may be put on signs, held up by children)

L: When we find ourselves in a tricky situation,
P: God is real!
L: When we find ourselves facing a difficult challenge,
P: God is with us!
L: When we need extra strength to face an obstacle,
P: God is strong!
L: When we are not sure where to turn,
P: God is in charge!
L: And when we know God loves us,
P: God is awesome!
L: Go now and live God's great adventure!

129 Who is in charge?

(can be used during elections or national holidays)

1: Who is in charge?
2: The world belongs to the Lord our God.
   The earth was shaped by God's hands.
P: God alone is Ruler.
1: Who is in charge?
2: Rulers come and rulers go.
   Some seek justice while others wreak havoc.
P: God alone is Ruler.
1: Who is in charge?
2: God's law is superior.
   The law of the Lord is our final authority.
P: God's love is our authority.
1: Who is in charge?
2: The love of God fulfills all the laws.
   God's law of love is the final testimony.
P: God's love is our authority.

1:   Is God's law of love in charge?
2:   God's law of love is our guide.
     God's law of love surrounds us.
P: **God alone is Ruler.**
     God's love is our authority.
All: *We worship the God who is in charge.*
       We worship the God of love.

130 God's reign through all generations

(can be used for a patriotic holiday)

We believe in God's reign—past, present, and future.
We believe God preserved our spiritual ancestors.
    The Hebrews were set free from Egypt.
    Jesus was raised from the dead.
    The Gentiles received the Holy Spirit.
    The church outlived the Empire.
We believe God's reign is now.
    We have been led through our own Red Seas.
    Christ has saved us from death.
    The Church has been filled with diversity.
    The Church testifies to peace and justice.
We believe God's reign will be fulfilled.
    Victory over evil will be completed.
    The persecuted will receive justice.
    The righteous will receive eternal life.
    The day will come when there will be no hunger,
        no thirst, and no tears.
We believe God's dominion endures throughout all generations.

131 Christ the image of the invisible God
(based on Colossians 1:16)

L: In Christ we find the image of the invisible God.
All: *We believe in the One who bore the fullness of God.*
We believe in the One who bore the fullness of humanity.
In this reconciling union
    God has shown the power of love over sin and death;
    God has shown us the way to fullness of life.
We follow in faith.

132 I keep the Lord ever before me
(based on Psalm 16:8)

L: Because you are at my right hand, I will not be shaken.
P: **Only you can protect us.**
L: I have no confidence in ability, money, or power.
P: **Only you can protect us.**
L: The world changes and things disappear.
P: **Only you can protect us.**
L: People and worldly things can let us down.
P: **Our confidence rests in you, for only you can protect us.**

133 The battle of the two kingdoms
(based on Matthew 5:3-11)

1:   Blessed are the poor in spirit,
      for theirs is the kingdom of heaven.
2:   Renowned are the overconfident,
      for the world is their oyster.

1:   Blessed are those who mourn,
      for they will be comforted.

2: Self-sufficient are those who get on with it,
        for they don't need help.

1: Blessed are the meek,
        for they will inherit the earth.
2: Powerful are the self-assertive,
        for they will get their own way!

1: Blessed are those who hunger and thirst for righteousness,
        for they will be filled.
2: Superior are those who take advantage of opportunities;
        too bad for everyone else.

1: Blessed are the merciful,
        for they will receive mercy.
2: Advantaged are the ruthless,
        for nobody will get in their way!

1: Blessed are the pure in heart,
        for they will see God.
2: Well-connected are the corrupt,
        for they will get things done.

1: Blessed are the peacemakers,
        for they will be called children of God.
2: Notorious are the discontent,
        for they will make themselves known.

1: Blessed are those who are persecuted for righteousness
    sake,
        for theirs is the kingdom of heaven.
2: Safe are those who do not stir the waters,
        for their lives will remain convenient.

1: Blessed are you when people revile you and persecute
you and utter all kinds of evil against you falsely
on my account.

2: Just go with the flow. Better safe than sorry.

134 Baby steps

(inspired by John 3:1-17)

There is a time to be born and a time to die;
and this is a time to be born.

✓ So we turn to you, God of our life;
our times are in your hands.

✓ Help us to hold your hand,
to trust you with our life, our congregation, our future,
not so we might never die,
but so we might truly live through Christ and for Christ.

✓ Through your Holy Spirit's power
move us from warmth of the womb to real life.

Knowing that you will never leave us nor forsake us,
we offer you our baby steps, in faith,
trusting you to raise us with your Son,
in whose name we pray. Amen.

135 Many members, one body

(based on Romans 12:1-8; can be used for the offering)

L: Lord, you have formed us to be a people—
the body of Christ, at work in your world.

**P: We celebrate the gifts you have given us
to carry out the work of your kingdom.**

L: You have given your people many gifts.
You have called some to teach,
some to administer,
some to offer hospitality,
some to share the Good News,
some to heal.

P: You have given each of us a gift.
We offer ourselves—our gifts, our time,
our energy, our resources—to you. Amen.

136 Lead lives worthy of the Lord

(based on Colossians 1:1-14)

L: As we grow in the knowledge of the Lord
and bear witness to the grace of God—
P: **may we lead lives worthy of the One
who rescues us from darkness.**
L: As we bear fruit in every good work
and prepare to endure everything in patience—
P: **may we lead lives worthy of the One
who redeems and forgives.**
L: As we hope in the word of truth
and gain spiritual wisdom and understanding—
P: **may we lead lives worthy of the One of glorious power.**

137 Love them as you have loved me

(based on John 17:23)

L: God of unity, hear our prayers …
P: **We give ourselves to each other
and pray that our humility
will reveal faith to all we meet.**
L: God of unity, hear our prayers …
P: **We give ourselves to you
and pray that our commitment
will speak hope to all we meet.**
L: God of unity hear our prayers …
P: **We give ourselves to our world
and pray that our service
will make known your love to all we meet. Amen.**

138 Walk in newness of life

(based on Romans 6:1-11)

L: Don't be afraid of the people to whom God is sending you.

P: What God says to you in the dark, tell in the light.

L: What you hear whispered, shout from the housetops.

All: God knows everything,
      even the number of hairs on your head.

L: For we are no longer buried with Christ

P: but united with Christ in the great resurrection,
      freed from sin and death,

All: raised to the glory of God,
      alive to God in Christ Jesus.

139 Given voice

1:   Who are you that have been given voice?

2:   Our name is Eve—
      garden resident, eater of fruit,
      female image of God.
      We are *created*.

3:   Who are you that come speaking and singing?

4:   Our name is Deborah,
      truth-speaker, mother of faith-bodies,
      singer of praise to the Lord God of Israel.
      We have *authority*.

2:   Our name is Lydia,
      church-builder and Christ-proclaimer
      in the absence of temple,
      in the presence of oppression,
      in the power of the Spirit.
      We are *empowered*.

1:   Who are you that come seeking forgiveness?

4: Our names are Potiphar's wife and Lot's wife.
    We are manipulators, liars,
        avoiders of personal responsibility,
        fists closed tightly around earthly treasures and names.
    We are *sinners*.

3: Who are you that come to be healed?

2: Our name is Bathsheba and our name is Leah,
        overpowered and victimized,
        objectified and silenced.
    We are *wounded*.

4: Our name is "hemorrhaging woman"
        biologically outcast,
        prohibited from participating
        in the dance and prayer of life;
        lonely and in need of the Cloak's fringe.
    We are *bound*.

3: Who are you that come, anyway?
    Who are you that are so filled with hope?

1: We are those who give praise to God,
        the Creator and Redeemer of all,
        who invites us into God's life and presence
        and says, "Do not fear"—

2: the one who offers his whole robe,
        who touches unconditionally,
        who nourishes and restores life.

3: We are those who cry out to God
        for forgiveness, mercy and grace.
    We cry out for courage
        to return our prayer-answers to their source.

1: We are those who have been given voice
        to shout and pray and sing
        names of thankfulness and trust,
        freedom and comfort, forgiveness and joy.

4: We are God's creatures who, with all creation,
        give praise and honor and glory
        to the everlasting triune God.

140 Building upside down

Father of all nations,
    who mothers us and labors in our deliverance,
    you build up the kingdom of heaven
    by constructing it upside down.
You train us as leaders,
    teaching us to imitate you in service.
You provide us wilderness food, drink, and sleep,
    extending the journey.
You know our suffering
    and you touch our weakness in love.
You ask as many questions of us as we ask of you.
You demonstrate your divinity by example—as a fully
    human man.
O Lord of peace and paradox, strengthen our faith.
Make us truly alive in you.
In the name of the Father, Son, and Holy Spirit we pray.
Amen.

Offering

141 Celebration of Life

(in the spirit of Psalm 133)

How good and pleasant it is
    when we share our gifts of money
   to further the way of love, hope, and justice
    in this community, and on earth.
May our offerings now be received
    in celebration of life, here and around the world.

142 Jesus guides our giving

Jesus is our peace.
Jesus' way guides who we are, what we do,
    and the way we give of ourselves.
May our tithes and offerings be given
    in joyful response to God's love.

143 God of abundance

God of abundance,
   all the things we have were yours before they were ours—
    your gifts to bring us joy and to meet our need.
Let them now become our gifts to others
    to bring them joy and to meet their need.

May we live so that others may have what we have
for Jesus' sake, Amen.

144 Most generous Spirit

All that we are and all that we have,
are gifts from you, most generous Spirit.
Unclench our hands from grasping,
free our hearts from the need of having,
and channel our work into sharing
your generosity among all your children. Amen.

145 Love God more than these

Money, O God, has the power
to capture our hearts,
to raise our anxiety,
and to make us hungry for more and more.
And so we bring you our money as an act of worship.
Release us from the seductive power of this false god.
Free us to generosity!
With these gifts we declare
that you are Lord of all,
and that we love you more than these.

146 Big things and small things

Generous God, we thank you for all you have given us:
For the big things—
the universe, the earth, the land and the sea.
For the beauty we see around us every day—
the goodness and love we know in family and friends.
For the gift of salvation through the resurrection
of Jesus Christ.

We thank you for the small things—
    the pleasure we have when we accomplish a task;
    the thoughtful word we receive at just the right time.
Accept the gifts we offer today, big and small,
    as tokens of our appreciation. Amen.

√√147 Without money and without price

Our giving God,
    you have called us to come, buy, and eat—
    without money and without price.
You have invited us to feast at your abundant table—
    where our thirst is quenched and our hunger is satisfied.
Now it's our privilege to share from this abundance.
Bless these gifts to your work
    so that others will no longer be thirsty or hungry.
In the name of Jesus we pray, Amen.

148 God of eternal time and space

Gracious God of eternal time and space,
    the opportunity to share is a blessing
    for which we give thanks.
Your generous provision for our needs
    invites us to be generous in return.
Accomplish your purposes, we pray,
    through these gifts and through our lives. Amen.

149 Wonders and whispers

God speaks to us in wonders and whispers,
    in silence and Scripture,
    through the life, death, and resurrection of Jesus

Christ.

God's gifts are boundless.
May we respond fully and freely
with hearts and lives given to God.

150 Hundredfold

We give to you our best—
thirtyfold, sixtyfold, and a hundredfold.
Use these gifts to meet the physical and spiritual needs
in our congregation, our community, and our world.
In Jesus' name we pray, Amen.

151 You shower us

Generous, gracious God:
You bless us with life.
You sustain us, that we might live fully.
You shower us with gifts,
that we might share your abundance freely.
Accept our offerings of thanksgiving, love, and commitment.
We offer them so that your name may be glorified
and your love shared in this city and in this world.
In the name of your greatest gift, Jesus Christ, we pray. Amen.

152 Multiply our humble gifts

Great God, you are the giver of life and all that is good.
Accept our humble gifts and multiply them.
Accept our humble hearts and mold them.
Accept our humble lives and transform them,
that we might live in the power of the resurrection,
willing to risk all for your kingdom.
In the name of Jesus we offer these gifts,
and in the name of Jesus we pray. Amen.

153 Small gifts

Our Provider, accept these small gifts,
  tokens of our great love for you.
Multiply them to do your good work
  in this church and in your world. Amen.

Sending

154 Anointed to heal

(based on Acts 10:34-43 and Matthew 3:13-17)

Just as God anointed Jesus of Nazareth
    with the power of the Holy Spirit,
    so you are now anointed to do good
    and to heal all who suffer evil
God is with you;
    go, therefore, and be the good news of peace,
    through Jesus Christ, who is Lord of all.

155 Weekly closing prayer

May there be love and understanding
    in our hearts and in our world.
May peace and friendship offer shelter from life's storms.
May we be released from our deep fears
    and our fruitless guilt.
May we have the courage to speak truth
    against violence and suffering.

Guiding Spirit, bless our journey with these good companions,
    that we may be drenched with the longing for peace,
    to make justice blossom on earth. Amen.

156 In the Spirit of Jesus

Go in the Spirit of Jesus, who proclaimed God's loving care.
Where there is illness or injury,
   may there be healing.
Where there is loneliness and isolation,
   may there be companionship and renewed community.
Where there is conflict and broken relationship,
   may God's peace be restored.

157 Laborers in the field

The Lord of the harvest blesses you.
The Christ of the cross sends you into a needy world.
Go on your way—laborers in the field of God's kingdom.

158 Freedom

Through Jesus Christ, you are free
   to extend forgiveness and to be forgiven;
   to serve and to be served;
   to love and to accept love.
Go into your communities this week as a free people.

159 Light of Christ

Now may the light of Christ burn brightly within you,
   that the world may see and know
   the loving Source of all truth and light.

160 Overflow of grace

(based on Psalm 91:1-6, 1 Timothy 6:6-19)

May the Lord God, our Refuge and Fortress,
> pour upon us the abundant blessings of the Holy Spirit,
> that we may be rich in good works,
> and give from the overflow of grace
> that we have received in Jesus Christ.

Go now and live true life.

161 The song of Christ be sung

(based on 2 Thessalonians 3:13)

By your hands, may love be shared.
By your voice, may peace be spoken.
By your eyes, may beauty be seen.
By your ears, may truth be heard.
By your life, may the song of Christ be sung!

162 God of creation

Now may the God of creation,
> who has numbered all the hairs on your head
> and knows all the fish of the seas—
may this God fill you with all wisdom and insight,
> so that you may be blameless until the day of Christ,
> when all of creation will be reconciled to God
> > through God's Son, Jesus Christ.
To God be all glory, honor, majesty, and praise,
> both now and forevermore.

163 Living by faith
(based on Hebrews 11:3)

We go from here, sure of what we hope for
in a world that is not sure of anything.
We go, certain of what we do not see,
into a world where "seeing is believing."
We go, living by faith,
in a world created and loved by God.

164 Things above

Go in the joy of knowing
that since you have been raised in Christ,
your treasures are above!
Share this good news.

165 Triune God
(based on Romans 3:28)

In faith go, confident that
God the Maker is good and loving,
God the Savior is generous and giving, and
God the Spirit guides and comforts.
The triune God goes with you to do in your life
that which is beyond your ability to imagine.
Thanks be to God.

166 Take hold of peace
(based on Romans 11:31)

In all the earth, both far and near,
go forth, go forth, that all may hear.

In all the land extend a hand;
    take hold of peace that wrath may cease.
Let grace abound, let grace abound!

167 Words of mission

Let us leave this sacred place
    with renewed hope and imagination.
    (extinguish Christ candle)
The flame is not extinguished—
    for the light of God shines in you!
Go into the world
    and be a place and a people of welcome,
    signs of a new creation and of God's embracing love!

168 God's overarching love

May the love of God be
    above you in an overarching sky,
    beneath you in firm good earth,
    around you in life-giving air.
So may you be glad and rejoice wherever you go.

The Christian Year

Advent

169 Gathering

Come, God is calling,
    amid seasonal pressures and anticipations.
God's Spirit envelops us in a story,
    a story of accepting without knowing,
    of believing without answers.
May we, too, abandon our expectations
    and answer God's call with joy.

170 Gathering

L: In Advent God calls us to become new,
P: to make room for our own nativity,
    even when there is no room at the inn.
L: Where we are busy—
P: grant peace.
L: Where we are lost—
P: grant salvation.
L: Where we are sad—
P: grant joy.
L: Where we are bitter—
P: grant love.
L: May this be a time to hope for all these gifts of God.
All: Amen.

171 Invocation

We are waiting, O God.
We know you work wonders:
    you announce mysteries;
    you choose the surprising;
    you startle the unsuspecting;
    you keep hope, joy, and peace alive;
    you fulfill your promises.
May we not only know—
    may we also practice believing
    while we are waiting.

172 Invocation

Like a pregnant woman waiting for the birth of her baby,
    so we wait for you, O God.
Eager and anxious, we long for you.
We want our lives to be worthy of you.

Like a pregnant woman ever aware of new life
    growing within her,
    so we want to be ever aware of you.
Turn our minds and hearts toward you;
    attune us to new life forming in us. Amen.

173 Prayer

L: Amid our confusion, God calls us.
    We have so many questions and so few answers.
    Yet through our uncertainty you embrace us;
        you draw us close.
P: **May our hearts fill with joy as we enter your mystery.**

L: Amid our desires, God calls us.
We lose ourselves in our wants, and neglect our needs.
Yet through our yearning you engage us;
you draw us close.

P: **May our hearts fill with joy as we enter your mystery.**

L: Amid our weakness, God calls us.
We strive for independence and refuse to hear your voice.
Yet through our foolish pride you enlighten us;
you draw us close.

P: **May our hearts fill with joy as we enter your mystery.**

174 Confession

(Use with "Slowly turning, ever turning" (STJ 23).)

1: O God, you come to earth to show us how to love.
But there are those who are so cutting,
so overbearing, so rigid, so unjust.
They cause our hearts of compassion to freeze.
Turn us to the ways of your warming heart.
(sing stanza 1)

2: You come to earth to widen the circle.
But we cling so closely to our own points of view.
We try to manipulate things
to fit our narrow perspectives.
Turn us to the ways of your inclusive heart.
(sing stanza 2)

3: You come to earth to show us how to be fearless.
But we are so easily frightened,
of suffering, death, and loss.
Turn us, O God, to your healing heart,
(sing stanza 3)

All: *May the daybreak of your presence dawn upon us all.*
Amen.

175 Prayer

Mary's song—
    can we sing it on a bleak mid-winter midnight
    while we wait for good news
        and the wars just get worse
        and the children keep dying?
Is the Child winning the battle
    and we just can't see well enough?
But we can pray—that the hope of the world
    keeps being born in us
    and God will do the rest.

176 Prayer

Son of God, in the bleak midwinter
    when the light is dim
    and we wonder where you are,
    give us eyes to see the stars shine
    in the darkest night sky.
In the tiny fingers of a newborn baby,
    we find infinite hope.
In the shadows of our dreary existence,
    may we see you open your arms to receive us again.
Remind us that you come to us
    in the form of a child.
May we find you in the little places of our lives
    and in the poor ones where you dwell. Amen.

177 Response

L: Faithful God, we forget you.
    We confess our lack of faith.

Convict us of sin. Free us from our idolatry.
Save us from the gods of this land that so easily
    ensnare us.
In your mercy, hear your people.

P: **Redeem us, saving God.**

L: You invite us to rest in your faithfulness,
        yet we refuse and turn to our own gods,
        images of our own desires,
        human creations that give life to the evils
        hidden in our depths.

Save us from ourselves.
In your mercy, hear your people.

P: **Redeem us, saving God.**

L: We long to see you face-to-face.
Look upon us with favor and rescue your scattered sheep.
Gather all of us into your promised land,
    the home of your beloved Son.

May the Holy Spirit illumine a path of servanthood
    where we learn to see you in "the least of these."

For the greatest in your kingdom is the servant,
    the slain Lamb.

P: **Come Lord Jesus, Messiah,**
    long awaited promised One. Amen.

178 Benediction

Go now, like Mary,
    carrying within you what God has implanted this season,
    nurturing it with love
    and preparing to share it with the world.

Christmas Eve

read all **179** Gathering Prayer

1: O surprising and faithful God:
We have been waiting for this evening,
wondering about your coming.

2: Will you enter as a mighty ruler with an enormous army?
Will you arrive as an astute politician,
able to maneuver influential minds?

1: Will you rise to popularity as a charismatic dynamo,
with adoring fans in every corner of the world?

2: Or—is it true . . . that you come
in the most helpless life form . . .
as a newborn infant—poor, vulnerable, dependent?
How can this be?
How can your reign possibly begin
with a messy birth in a humble hut?

1: But here you come, with the gasping cry of new birth,
and you invite us to re-imagine God-power
from the downside-up.

2: Thank you for inviting us here into your birthing room.
Thank you for finding a deeper, more enduring way.

All: *Let your birth cries penetrate our minds and hearts.*
Bless this celebration, and may we, like Mary,
continue to ponder all these things.
In gratitude and with wonder we pray. Amen.

180 Prayer *at mealtime*

Incarnate God, this night we remember when the soles of
your feet touched the earth where we dwell. We recall
your coming into the lowliest of dwellings, a stable for cattle.
We give thanks for your coming as an infant, taking on all

the qualities and characteristics of humans, providing a fuller picture of who you are and what we might become through your transforming power and love.

Amid the fanfare of this season and all the distractions of commerce; amid the heightened expectations from others and the inordinate pressures we place on ourselves— empower us to hear and receive the good news of great joy given on that sacred night to the humble shepherds. Awaken within us the uninhibited delight of a child, the energy of youth, and the capacity of the elderly to see the bigger picture of what you are up to in this world.

Let this celebration be but a foretaste of the greater gifts you wish for us each day and through the coming year. In the name of the One named Jesus, whom we call Emmanuel, Amen.

181 Readers theatre

(can be used with candle lighting)

1: On this night, ordinary things become extraordinary.
2: An animal shelter becomes a sanctuary.
3: A journey becomes a beginning.
4: Field workers become the first to see Christ.

2: On this night, ordinary things become extraordinary.
4: Scandal and embarrassment are transformed.
3: Fear is soothed.
1: The birth of a baby is celebrated.

3: On this night, ordinary things become extraordinary.
1: A light comes into the darkness.
4: It touches those around it,
2: and ignites the skies with heavenly voices.

4: On this night ordinary things become extraordinary.
3: And on this night extraordinary things become ordinary.
2: On this night, God becomes ordinary.
1: On this night, we can hold love in our hands.

Christmas

182 Gathering

("glory" can be recited by alternate sides)

P: Glory, glory, glory!
L: We can live fully in this day! God is here. God has come.
What a surprise! Impossible to imagine!
P: Glory, glory, glory!
L: We can cry out to God in anger, loneliness,
pain, and sorrow.
What faithfulness! Impossible to imagine!
P: Glory, glory, glory!
L: We have been restored;
our weeping has been turned to shouts of joy
What restoration! Impossible to imagine!
P: Glory, glory, glory!
L: We have been invited to be heirs of God's kingdom
through rebirth.
What an invitation! Impossible to imagine!
P: Glory, glory, glory!
L: God most high, ordinary baby boy,
Rod of Jesse, Rose of Sharon!
What an extraordinary beginning!
P: Thanks be to God!

183 Prayer for those who grieve

*Prior to the prayer, worshippers may place rocks or
candles near the manger or at the foot of the cross.*

Blessed incarnate God,
    we have entered a season of celebration.
The wait is over; the Son is born.
But for some, this is also a season of sadness.
We remember loved ones who are not with us:
    those who are far from home,
    who are lonely or estranged,
    who are disappointed or needy;
    those who are ill and in need of healing,
    who are waiting for death,
    or who have already passed through.
As we remember, fill our hearts with your love.
Renew our hope through your holy presence
    in our laughter
    and in our tears.
✓ In you there is new life, a new future.
✓ Let us celebrate in truth, with our whole being. Amen.

Epiphany

184 Gathering

(based on Isaiah 60:1-6 and Psalm 72)

1:   Get up! Lift your eyes!
      See the shining! Your light has come;
         the glory of the Lord has risen upon you.
    2:   Though vast darkness covers our planet,
         now God has appeared—
         like a floodlight revealing this Christ child.

3:   The treasures of the magi
          are gifts of mere earthly kings
          compared to the Gift that is now made known
          to all creation.

1:   Messiah, Christ,

2:   Prince of peace,

3:   Defender of the poor:

All: *You offer mercy to all, you free us from oppression.*

1:   Our souls, tattered by the world, become radiant.

2:   Our hearts thrill and rejoice!

3:   We dare to utter the hope of the promise:

All: *We taste at last the year of Jubilee.*

185 Confession

Our baptized Lord:
As a people we cry to you;
      our tears form your baptismal river.
Lead us back to water and womb,
      that we may grow in your likeness:
      belonging to your body of believers,
      fulfilling your purposes and not our own.
Come, Creator, Lover, Sustainer. Amen.

186 Prayer

L: Lord God, we know you are here among us,
      enter the shadows in our hearts.

P: Lord of Light, enter our darkness.

L: For those who have traveled through the storms of life,
      for those who are still on the road,

P: Lord of Light, enter our darkness.

L: For those bearing gifts in your name,
      for those who feel they have no gift to bring,

P: **Lord of Light, enter our darkness.**
L: For those who are carrying their loved ones,
　　　 for those who need to be loved and carried,
P: **Lord of Light, enter our darkness.**
L: For those who are our leaders,
　　　 for those who are afraid to lead,
P: **Lord of Light, enter our darkness.**
L: For those who are strangers in a new place,
　　　 for those who are strangers in a place called home,
P: **Lord of Light, enter our darkness.**
L: Lord God, we know you are here among us,
　　　 enter the shadows in our hearts,
All: *Lord of Light, enter our darkness.*

187 Offering

Invitation
The Magi saw his star at its rising
　　 and knew that God's light had come.
They responded by offering their time, energies, gifts, and
　　 praise.
May we respond to God's light just as fully and freely.
　　 (receive the offering)

Prayer
Radiant and Holy God,
　　　 these baskets that we lift before you
　　　 do not hold gold or frankincense or myrrh.
But they do hold gifts that represent our love, our
　　 commitment, and our praise.
Accept them as we bow before you.
May they be used to reveal your radiant glory to all.
In the name of Jesus, we pray. Amen.

Transfiguration Sunday

188 Gathering

The Spirit of the Lord is upon us.
And where the Spirit is, there is freedom.
All of us, with uncovered faces,
 seeing the glory of the Lord,
 are being transformed from glory to glory.
The Spirit of the Lord is upon us.
Let us revel in God's presence.

189 Affirmation

(based on 2 Kings 2:1-12, Psalm 50:1-6, Mark 9:2-9)

L: Elijah ascends to heaven in the midst of fire,
P: and from the witness of Elisha, God shines forth!
L: Jesus is transfigured in dazzling white,
P: and from the witness of Peter, James, and John,
   God shines forth!
L: God declares justice,
P: and from the witness of heaven and earth,
   God shines forth!
L: God covenants with the faithful,
P: and from our witness, God shines forth!
L: God speaks and in profound ways summons the earth.
P: God comes and does not keep silent!

190 Prayer

Loving Mother-Father God,
 thank you for gathering us together—
 all of us beautiful, bumbling followers of your Son.

As we hear anew the story of sleepy Peter, James, and John
>with radiant Jesus on the mountain,
>awaken us to the voice of your Spirit
>and to the bright wonder of your vision for our lives
>in this community and all of creation.

Like Peter, we are often preoccupied with the mundane,
>or we get lost in the clouds.

We miss the point. We don't see the big picture
>of who you are,
>what you're doing,
>and what you are saying.

Forgive us, we pray.
>*(pause)*

Knowing that you delight in forgiveness
>and care about our preoccupations and dreams,
>we pour our joys and concerns into your hands.

Hear and receive our spoken and unspoken prayers, O God.
>*(pause for spoken and silent prayers.)*

Knowing that you transform illness to health,
>confusion to clarity, violence to peace, ashes to beauty,
>we thank you for hearing our prayers.

Open our awareness this day to your Spirit dancing among us.
Amen.

191 Benediction

(cup hands behind ears at the beginning)

Hear, O people of *(location)*:
The Lord Our God, the Lord is Three-in-One!
As you go from this place, may the Divine Dancing Three
>sweep you off your feet and dance with you
>through the coming days.

May God surprise you with soul-penetrating rhythms
>and dare you to try new steps as you go from this place.

Ash Wednesday

192 Gathering

The path that lies before us is not an easy one.
To reach the place of new life
    we must first wander through shadows of death.
Solemn with ash-stained skin,
    we go out on our Lenten travels.
√ Yet our journey is not solitary.
We go in the company of the Man of Sorrows,
    following in his path,
    for it is our way home.

193 Prayer of confession

Holy God, we confess
    our attachment to earthly treasures,
    our hypocrisy and hidden idols,
our temptation to forsake you,
    to take the "easy" way out.
√√ Grant us grace and mercy to let go
    of all that keeps us from you.
Forgive us in Jesus' name we pray. Amen.

194 Beatitudes prayer

("Ubi caritas" (HWB 452) is an appropriate sung response.)

God of Lenten journeys, we look to the empowering Jesus
who loves the poor, challenges the self-assured and lifts up
the lowly. May we be guided by your Spirit.
(sung response)

We look to the vulnerable Jesus who weeps over Jerusalem, grieves the death of friends, and comforts those who mourn. May we be filled with your compassion.
(sung response)

We look to the humble Jesus who stoops to wash disciples' feet and welcomes the children to receive his blessing. May we, in humility, point to your glorious love.
(sung response)

We look to the just Jesus who overturns the tables of the money-changers, challenges corrupt authorities, and transforms the lives of the oppressed. May we hunger and thirst for your justice.
(sung response)

We look to the merciful Jesus who welcomes sinners to his table, heals diseases, and touches those who never are touched. May we reflect such mercy.
(sung response)

We look to the praying Jesus who teaches prayer and leaves the crowd to encounter you in the desert and on the mountaintop. May we attend to your presence and grow in maturity of faith.
(sung response)

We look to the peacemaking Jesus who chooses humility over dominance, servanthood over force. May we embrace your message of reconciliation and love.
(sung response)

We look to the bold Jesus, who suffers because of the path he walks and rejoices in the good news he proclaims. May we know your joy and passion as we walk this Lenten journey.
(sung response)

God of Lenten journeys, we claim the Beatitudes as our
guide and affirmation as we walk with our eyes set on
Jesus, seeking faithfulness on this road to his cross. Amen.

Lent

195 Gathering

God desires to gather us as a hen gathers her chicks.
So come! Leave behind your distractions,
    and crawl under the sheltering wing of God's care.
Come and worship our loving God!

196 Invocation

(inspired by John 3)

Redeeming God, you loved the world so much
    that you sent your Holy Word into our darkness.
Through the love and gentleness of Jesus
    we are born anew and nourished to life eternal.
We worship you in gratefulness and adoration. Amen.

197 Invocation

God, our loving Parent and Guide,
    you know our waywardness as prodigal children.
Sometimes we wonder: will you welcome us,
    or will you turn us away?
Help us recognize you as our true source of forgiveness. Amen.

198 Confession

Into our bottomless anxiety,
    into our fearful bewilderment,
    our fretful minds and aching hearts,
you come to rebuild and repair and restore.

You walk right into our hand-wringing,
    and with calming serenity
you breathe peace.

Soak your song of hope
    into our dust-dry lives
and free us to endless love
    in Jesus Christ. Amen.

199 Response

(based on John 4:5-42)

Renewing God, you know when we are spiritually
    dehydrated.
Pour into us your Holy Spirit that refreshes.
Save our very lives so that we may do your will
    and be your church for your glory and praise,
    by the power of your risen Son. Amen.

200 Prayer of confession

L: We pray with the psalmist:
    "I have become like a broken vessel.
    "I trust in you, O Lord. Deliver me."
All: *Healing God, we come as we are.*
    (hands held cupped in front of self)

We acknowledge our brokenness.
(hands overlapping, shielding face, head down)
We look to you for restoration.
(hands scoop down and arch up, face upturned)
L: As broken vessels, we need reassuring signs
    of your blessing and promise.
  Our world is hurting; our lives are often chaotic.
  The future seems uncertain; we falter in fear and doubt.
  (pause for silent review)
All: **Restore and bless us.**
  Heal us and make us whole
  that we may reflect your image more truly in the world.
  Amen.

Words of assurance
God remembers the divine covenant with us
  (trace an arc-like rainbow in the air)
and brings us wholeness and peace.

201 Confession and reconciliation

(in unison)

Our faith is so small, O God.
We often find ourselves asking, like Nicodemus,
  "How can these things be?"
  Help us to face our unbelief.
  Teach us to accept what life brings.
  Inspire us to be a compassionate presence in the world,
    and to receive anew the rebirth of water and Spirit
    offered to us in Jesus. Amen.

202 Prayer of confession and assurance

L: How often I desire to gather you together
    as a hen gathers her brood under her wings.

I want to shelter you in the day of trouble,
    and hide you under the cover of my tent.
But you turn away!

P: **O Lord, be merciful!**
Do not cast your servants away in anger.
Do not forsake us now.
You alone have been our helper.

L: Then come! Seek God's face.
Wait for the Lord and let your heart take courage.

P: **O Lord, your face alone do we seek.**
Our desire is to live with you all the days of our lives.

L: Then be strong and take heart!
For you will see the goodness of the Lord
    in the land of the living.

203 Sending

Go out with confidence,
    standing firm in the Lord
    because you are loved forever.

Holy Week

204 Palm Sunday affirmation

L: The crowds cheer and shout:

1-4: Hosanna in the highest.
Blessed is he who comes in the name of the Lord!

L: They wave palm branches
    and spread their garments out on the road
    as Jesus enters Jerusalem.
The whole city joins in to give Jesus

1:   a hero's welcome

2:     a ticker-tape parade
3:     a royal reception
4:     a citywide party.
L: But the cheers are shallow—
         the celebration is short -lived.
       In the background the chief priests, the scribes,
           the Pharisees, the Sadducees and Herodians
1:     are green with envy
2:     and red with anger.
L: They set their traps with tricky words,
3:       and buy their spy with thirty coins,
4:       preparing to kill the Son of God.
L: Today is Palm Sunday: a day of paradox.
1:   This day the king rides to the capital on a lowly colt.
2:   This day he cries at his royal reception,
3:   This day the cheers briefly hold back the drumbeats of
         doom.
L: This day we take our places in the crowd.

205 Palm Sunday prayer

O reigning God:
We give you thanks for your son, Jesus
     who rode in triumph into the city of Jerusalem.
He was honored and acclaimed as king.
We thank you that he came, showing us the reign of God,
     not as an earthly king, but as a servant to many,
   obedient to pain, rejection, and defilement,
   to complete your plan of salvation for all.
Let our words proclaim Christ as King of our lives
     and confess him as Lord,
       to the glory of your name. Amen.

206 Lenten Tenebrae*

(begins with a ring of six lit candles around a Christ candle)

L: When we are unkind to each other,
       the world becomes a darker place.
       (extinguish one candle)
P: **Jesus taught us to love each other.**

L: When we want everything for ourselves,
       the world becomes a darker place.
       (extinguish one candle)
P: **Jesus taught us to share with others.**

L: When we scare or bully others,
       the world becomes a darker place.
       (extinguish one candle)
P: **Jesus taught us that love is better than fear.**

L: When we are jealous of others,
       the world becomes a darker place.
       (extinguish one candle)
P: **Jesus taught us contentment.**

L: When we lie,
       the world becomes a darker place.
       (extinguish one candle)
P: **Jesus taught us honesty.**

L: People's hatred, greed, selfishness, jealousy, and
       dishonesty placed Jesus on the cross.
       (extinguish one candle)
P: **For Jesus' friends, the world seemed a dark place.**

---

* *tenebrae*: Latin for "shadows" and used for gathering shadows of
Maundy Thursday or Good Friday. This litany works well with children and in intergenerational settings.

L: In the darkness, Jesus said, "O God, forgive them,
    for they don't know what they're doing."
    (extinguish Christ candle)

Option: continue on Easter morning

L: On that first Easter, God raised Jesus to life
    and the world became a brighter place!
    (light Christ candle)
P: Jesus' love came to lighten the world.

L: Jesus' love shines through each of us
    and makes the world a brighter place.
    (light one candle)
P: Jesus' love shines through loving actions and words.

L: When we share with those who have less,
    the world becomes a brighter place.
    (light one candle)
P: Jesus wants us to share.

L: When we trust God and are no longer afraid,
    the world becomes a brighter place.
    (light one candle)
P: Jesus wants us to trust.

L: When we are content with what we have,
    the world becomes a brighter place.
    (light one candle)
P: Jesus will supply our needs.

L: When we are honest, the world becomes a brighter place.
P: Jesus helps us be truthful.
    (light one candle)

L: When Jesus lives in us,
         the world becomes a brighter place.
         (light one candle)
√√ **P: Alleluia! Christ is risen.**

207 Maundy Thursday invocation

Jesus, be present at our tables,
     at our basins,
     and in our hearts as we pray with one another.
May your Spirit move among us in water, soup, and bread,
     so that we might become your living body
     and reflect your holy passion for love and justice.
In your name we pray. Amen.

208 Maundy Thursday prayer

  1:   Jesus, Son of Mary,
  2:   Jesus, Son of God,
1&2:   Speak to us in the silence.
  1:   We taste bread and wine—
         common elements of a common meal;
         one cup, one loaf, uncommon sustenance.
  2:   We consider the servant symbol—
         a kneeling slave holding towel and basin,
         a royal posture.
  1:   We hear the cock crow at daybreak—
         reminder of lurking denial,
         forerunner of repentance.
  2:   We touch spikes of thorn—
         twisted circle of pain,
         a piercing halo.
1&2:   Jesus, speak to us in the silence.

209 Good Friday reading

He hangs newly suspended,
   his stretched arms screaming
   new messages to his reeling brain.

Out of that pain
   of that high abyss
   spills a continuing mutter,
   a private pleading,
   a cosmic grace.

210 Good Friday prayer and sending

Prayer
Holy God,
   the earth waits in silence:
   we tremble before your throne.
On this day we see and feel the immensity of your love
   and our own unworthiness.
Open our hearts now to receive your redeeming grace.
We pray in the name of our Savior. Amen.

Blessing
We have seen the suffering of our Savior;
   we have marveled at the abundance of God's grace.
Now go forth as loved and forgiven people
   and share the love of Christ in the world.

211 Sabbath silent
(can be used at the end of a Good Friday service)

Of the ground are we,
   and the breath of the Son.

Now dying he takes
  our breath away.

For how can the death of
  him who is
  Ground and Source,
  First and Last,
  End and Beginning,
  All in all, not be
  the death of all things?
Our Maker and Son dies
  and thus entombs
  all generations in his passing.
"It is finished."

Yet in this tomb none other is laid:
  not from sin's woes but for them.
So dies, unto Death's demise,
  the One who all things made.
The Ground in the ground is laid,
  unmade, to make all things new.

Strangely like his former rest!
Then he rested in a garden of trees.
Now he rests in a garden of tombs.
Then he descended among the living
  to walk with them in the cool of day.
Now he descends among the dead
  to walk with them in the fire of night–
  again to meet the tempter!
To the garden of trees
  came the tempter for plunder.

From the garden of tombs,
  the Lord goes down
  to plunder the tempter's lair.

O special and Holy Sabbath!
In the silence of Seven,
    no Word be spoken,
    no Bread be broken.
In the quiet of his planting
    hearken to the ground and
    hear the Devil's wail, whose
    Hell is abandoned.
And through the day of Sabbath
    silent be on guard all we baptized,
    and you who prepare—beware
    the vagabond tempter now
    lonely, homeless, desperate.

'Tis a day of watching
    bounded by sleeps
    and the first is now upon us.
Descend with him,
    that you may rise.
Rest in peace.
Sleep in the death of the Lord
    as in thine own.

To rouse us from the second,
    interrupted slumber,
    his breath again will beckon—
"Awake, O Sleeper!"—
    for soon and soon,
    a new world,
    new heavens,
    new gardens to tend.

Easter

212 Gathering

We gather today
> to celebrate the resurrection
> of our Lord and Savior Jesus Christ
> and to proclaim that life and love
> have triumphed
> and will triumph
> over the violence and death that fill our
> world and our newspapers today.
As we worship in these safe surroundings
> may we remember our sisters and brothers around
> > the world
> who dare to declare the power of the resurrection
> even in the face of persecution, war, poverty,
> and threat of death.
As God strengthens them
> may God also make us bold
> to live as people who have been made new
> by the power of the resurrection.
Christ is risen!
Christ is risen indeed!

213 Gathering

L: Spring is risen!
P: Spring is risen indeed!

L: Hope is risen!
P: Hope is risen indeed!

L: Christ is risen!
All: Alleluia! Christ is risen indeed!

214 Gathering

L: This is Good News!
The rulers passed judgment,
finding him worthy of crucifixion and humiliation.
✓ But he refused to retaliate and was raised from the dead.
The principalities and powers said,
"No, this cannot be God's true Son."
But God said, "Yes, this is my Son,
in whom I am well pleased."

All: *Alleluia! His cross and resurrection are God's defeat of evil!*

215 Gathering

Mary came grieving to the tomb.
She lost her kindest friend,
the most generous, caring person she knew,
to an untimely, violent death.

Mary came grieving to the tomb.
Her heart, her body were
heavy with the weight of sorrow,
numb with the shock of her loss.

Mary came grieving to the tomb.
And she could not have known that
what she would find there was
resurrection and life.

Many of us come grieving this morning.
We may feel heavy with the weight of sorrow.
We may feel numb with the shock of loss.
But we know of Mary's joy.
We have heard that her hope was realized.

Come, let us celebrate together,
expecting
resurrection and life.

(216) Gathering

(based on 1 Corinthians 15:4)

L: We are here today because
        the weeping Mary of Magdala once said:
P: "I have seen the Lord!"
L: We are here on this Easter morning because
        Jesus still comes into our locked spaces and says:
P: "Peace be with you. Receive the Holy Spirit."
L: We are here today like doubting Thomas who finally cried:
P: "My Lord and my God!"
L: We are here like Peter, tempted to forget the call of Jesus:
P: "I'm going fishing."
L: We are here this morning because of Jesus,
        who asks us face-to-face:
P: "Do you truly love me?"
L: We gather here to whisper timidly:
P: "Yes, Lord, you know that we love you."
L: We are here as a congregation only because
        many faithful disciples have listened to Jesus' words:
All: *"Do not be afraid. Do not be afraid!*
          Go and tell, 'Jesus has been raised!'"

217 Response

She came for the work of death.
No joy, only sorrow and tender obligation.
On a dark early morning,
after a long and terrible Sabbath,
she came—

no hope of the unexpected, no excitement,
only resignation—
this common woman,
whose only vocation today was grief,
made holy by the Holy One himself,
seeking her Lord,
entombed in death,
sealed away by those who feared his life.

Now her death-work, interrupted
by a rolled-away rock, folded linens.
Later, a would-be gardener
clearly calling out:
"Death's work is done."

And from her lips ring forth
the first proclamation—
echoing through the canyons of time
and still shaking the ground on which we stand:
"I have seen the Lord."

218 Prayer

As brother sun shines down on us this morning, we remember
    that sister moon was just here.
We remember in this sunlight and in this brightness, the cold
    and the darkness of the night we have just been through.
We remember the darkness, when night bent down and
    covered our unready eyes.
We remember the cold, when the rays of the sun no long
    held us tight in their embrace.
We remember the hopelessness, when darkness seemed to
    have the final word.
And we remember the pain, when distant stars reminded us
    of our own Star, our own life-giving Sustainer, whom we
    were sure would never leave us.

But it did, and there was night, there was emptiness. And
weary with toil and tears, we turned from the western
horizon where we watched our love die, and we went
home with our hearts torn in two, and somehow, we slept.
And yet, we are here, in the sunlight; and we look back and
see the night with new eyes. The darkness, the cold, the
hopelessness, the pain were all real. But the cosmos was
pregnant with a new hope and a new life. We had to go
through those pains for today to happen.
Birthing is not easy, and the laments of Maundy Thursday
and Good Friday were the world's labor pains. The sun
had descended into the world and the world groaned
with the life which it knew it could not contain. When
we saw that descent, that fall, we wept bitterly.
But we were blind, for now the earth brings forth her joy!
The dawn has come, and the sun is risen!

219 Benediction

May hope in the Risen Christ sustain you.
May faith in the Risen Christ strengthen you.
May the joy of the Risen Christ radiate in your lives
today and in the days to come.
Go in the peace of new life. Amen.

220 Benediction

May things of joy, beauty, truth, and hope bloom in your life.
And if not bloom, then sprout.
And if not sprout, then take root
And if not take root, then be sown.

Ascension Day

221 Gathering

(based on Psalm 93, Psalm 47:6)

1:   The Lord is King,
2:   robed in majesty,
1:   girded with strength,
2:   more majestic than roaring waters
1:   and thundering waves!
2:   Let us sing praises to God;
1:   sing praises to our King!
All: Alleluia!

222 Benediction

(first part can be echoed by congregation line by line)

This same Jesus,
     who has been taken from you
     into heaven
     will come back
     in the same way you have seen him go
     into heaven.
Alleluia!
     (end echo)
L: Sisters and brothers,
     may the Lord fill you with the Holy Spirit
     as you go in peace to serve the Lord.
P: Thanks be to God.

(223) Sending

We will not let you go, ascending Jesus,
    unless you bless us.
Embrace us with your love;
    send us forth with your power.
Convince us that you will have the last word
    in our lives and in the world.
Sustain us in every risk we take for good. Amen.

Pentecost

224 Gathering

(based on Psalm 104)

All: **Lord, send down your Spirit,**
          and renew the face of the earth.
1:   Praise be to God! Mighty are God's works.
2:   The Lord gives life to the earth.
3:   The Lord cares for all creation
All: **We are filled with your abundance.**
1:   May the glory of the Lord shine forever.
2:   God looks on the earth and it trembles.
3:   The Lord touches the mountains and they smoke.
1:   Let us sing to the Lord while we live.
All: **Lord, send down your Spirit,**
          and renew the face of the earth.

225 Gathering

(lines before prayer can be echoed by congregation)

Do not leave the city,
    but wait for the gift
      my Father promised.

For John baptized you with water,
    but in a little while
    you will be baptized with the Holy Spirit.

It is not for you to know
    the day or the hour
    the Father has chosen by his own authority.
But you will receive power
    when the Holy Spirit comes upon you.
And you will be my witnesses—
    in the city,
    and in the countryside,
    and to the ends of the earth.

Prayer

O God, you have gathered us in to sing your mighty power.
You have loaned us our lives, and we are ever in your care.
There is no place that we can go but you are present there.
So we say, "Holy Spirit, come with power!
    We expect you this glad hour!"* Amen.

226 Invocation

We call upon your name, Lord,
    with a sense of expectation.
We know that like the early church,
    we may be amazed or perplexed
    at the power of the Holy Spirit moving in and upon us
    when we're all together in this place.
And so, as we take a deep breath, your breath,
    prepare us for what you would have us receive.
In the name of Jesus, the glorified One, we pray. Amen.

* From "Holy Spirit come with power" by Anne Neufeld Rupp (HWB 26).

227 Affirmation

L: From the beginning of time
    the Spirit of God encircled the earth—
1: moving with God over the face of the waters at creation,
2: going before the Israelites in a pillar of cloud and fire
        to the promised land;
1: interceding for Hannah as she prayed for a child,
2: writing psalms;
1: bringing visions to prophets;
2: moving the hearts of women and men to follow Jesus;
L: and coming as God's gift to us at Pentecost,
    in order to increase our access to God,
    that the church might be built up in love
    and grow to maturity.
All: *The God who gave us the gift of the Holy Spirit*
    is the God we have come to worship today.

228 Affirmation

(can also be used as a gathering piece)

Chaos at first.

Wind, fire, Spirit-flood
wash over them.

Chattering mouths
and clicking tongues
electrified
powered by this holy Energy
that courses through.

Now, plugged into the Divine,
they shout unknown praises,
and through the chattering clicking shouting growling den
    of unending praise
comes forth the only message that makes sense:
God is here.

229 Prayer

    L: Flash of the Spirit
           crash into our dry days.
✓ **P: Blast life into cold bones.**
    L: Red Flame of God,
           shot from the sun's center,
✓ **P: ignite us for your glory.**
    L: Holy Breath,
           fanning the four winds,
    P: carry us where you will.

230 Scripture reading with voice and violin*

(based on Acts 2:1-21)

    1:   When the day of Pentecost had come, they were all
         together in one place. And suddenly from heaven there
         came a sound like the rush of a violent wind, and it
         filled the house where they were sitting. *(violent wind
         sound)*

    2:   Divided tongues, as of fire, appeared among them, and
         a tongue rested on each of them. *(tongues of fire sound)*

    1:   All of them were filled with the Holy Spirit and began
         to speak in other languages, as the Spirit gave them
         ability. *(other languages sound)*

2: Now there were devout Jews from every nation living in Jerusalem. *(violent wind sound)*

1: And at this sound the crowd gathered and was bewildered, because each one heard them speaking in the native language of each. *(other languages sound)*

2: Amazed and astonished, they asked, "Are not all these who are speaking Galileans? And how is it that we hear, each of us, in our own native language? Parthians, Medes, Elamites, and residents of Mesopotamia, Judea and Cappadocia, Pontus and Asia, Phrygia and Pamphylia, Egypt and the parts of Libya belonging to Cyrene, and visitors from Rome, both Jews and proselytes, Cretans and Arabs—in our own languages we hear them speaking about God's deeds of power." *(other languages sound)*

1: All were amazed and perplexed, saying to one another, "What does this mean?" *(tongues of fire sound)*

2: But others sneered and said, "They are filled with new wine." But Peter, standing with the eleven, raised his voice and addressed them,

3: Men of Judea and all who live in Jerusalem, let this be known to you, and listen to what I say. Indeed, these are not drunk, as you suppose, for it is only nine o'clock in the morning. No, this is what was spoken through the prophet Joel: *(violent wind sound)*

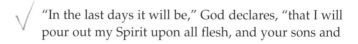 "In the last days it will be," God declares, "that I will pour out my Spirit upon all flesh, and your sons and

The violin creates three distinct sound patterns: **the violent wind with low and high tones; **the tongues of fire** sound suggests both miracle and curiosity; and **the other languages** sound is rich with multiple voices (double stops) perhaps using harmony.*

your daughters shall prophesy, and your young men
shall see visions, and your old men shall dream dreams.
(other languages sound)

"Even upon my slaves, both men and women, in those
days I will pour out my Spirit; and they shall prophesy.
(tongues of fire sound)

"And I will show portents in the heaven above and signs
on the earth below, blood, and fire, and smoky mist. The
sun shall be turned to darkness and the moon to blood,
before the coming of the Lord's great and glorious day.
Then everyone who calls on the name of the Lord shall
be saved."
(violent wind sound)

231 Prayer

God of surprising power,
we gather on this day of wind and fire.
Just as your movement shakes our foundations,
so too your wisdom inspires us beyond all we can
imagine.
Gather us,
release us from our fears,
stir new hope in our hearts,
and send us into the world,
May our lives be lifted by your breath
and our service set ablaze by your love. Amen.

232 Pentecost sending

All: *We go into a world of God's wondrous works and wisdom.*
   May we go as stewards of land and sea and all creatures.

> *Loving and sharing with others on the way,*
> *singing praises to the Lord.*

L: May our meditations be pleasing to God
and our lives rejoice in God's song.
Go in grace and peace.

Trinity Sunday

233 Invocation

L: God in Trinity, you have revealed yourself to us
as Maker of all things seen and unseen,
Giver of all good things.

**P: You have offered yourself for us
in Jesus Christ, our Redeemer.**

L: You have poured yourself out through the Holy Spirit,
to comfort and to guide.

P: We thank you and we praise you.

L: We gather to worship you and to wrestle
with the mystery of your self-revealing love.

**P: Open our hearts, our minds, our souls
to your movement among us.**

L: O God of Mystery, you bring us to life,
call us to freedom,
and move between us with such love.

**P: May we so participate in the dance of your Trinity
that our lives will resonate with you,
now and forever. Amen.**

234 Offering

Invitation

We are a richly blessed people,
    commissioned in the name of the Father and of the Son
    and of the Holy Spirit
      to bring forth the reign of mercy, peace, and justice—
      the very reign of God.
Sharing freely from all that God has provided—
    this is our act of thanksgiving and faithfulness.
Let us bring our offerings to God.
    (receive the offering)

Prayer

Holy and gracious One, Giver of all good things,
    for your abundance and unfailing mercy,
    we give you thanks.
Jesus Christ, our Redeemer,
    for your death on the cross
    and your life-giving resurrection,
    we give you thanks and praise.
Holy Spirit, Giver of life,
    for your indwelling presence
    and for the ways you both comfort and disturb us,
    we give you thanks and praise and glory.
God in Trinity, accept these gifts of love.
To you be glory and praise, now and forever. Amen.

235 Trinity offering

Invitation

From God, the Creator,
    we have received our very being and all that we have.
From Jesus, the Son,
    we have received our salvation and our commission.

From the Holy Spirit
  we have received God's truth and God's power.
Let us offer our gifts of thanksgiving.
  (receive the offering)

Prayer
By your love—celebrated in your Word, seen in your Son,
    brought near by your Spirit—
  we know you, blessed God.
With gratitude and in awe, we thank you
    for your care and your presence.
Accept these gifts of love and praise.
May they bring glory to the One who made us,
    to Christ who saved us,
    and to the Spirit who keeps us in faith. Amen.

All Saints' Day or Eternity Sunday

236 Prayer

(can be used at a funeral service)

Eternal Spirit of love, you are our home,
    our dwelling place at the heart of the universe.
Your light endows everything with life:
    light of each grateful morning,
    light of the infinite starry night,
    light jumping from human synapse to human synapse
    in sparkling array of intelligence and hope and joy.
Your light endows everything with life.
We thank for your light in the life of [*deceased person*], Hugo
    for the joy s/he brought to her/his family,
    for the liveliness of her/his place on this earth.

We give thanks for her/his life,
> which has joined the chorus of morning and evening song
> and the stories of so many touched by her/his life.

Today, we lift up and bless her/his memory
> and her/his place in eternity. Amen.

237 Prayer

(names of the deceased can be read before or after this prayer)

L: Ever-living God,
> the generations pass before you.

Your way is love,
> and your nature is compassion.

Today we remember those who lived
> and labored and loved among us.

We are here in the land of the dying,
> recalling those who have crossed to the land of
> > the living.

P: **Their memory is a blessing forever.**

L: We call to mind the great and the good,
> the long-suffering and the self-forgetful,
> those whose names are cherished,
> and those who died as though they had never been.

Wise and courageous in their words,
> they were just and loving in their deeds.

P: **Their memory is a blessing forever.**

L: We thank you for your boundless love in Christ,
> for his resurrection from the dead,
> and for your Spirit, the Comforter who never
> > leaves us.

P: **Your presence is a blessing forever.**

L: O God, our Breath,
We are yours: our help is in you.
Our hope is in your promise.

P: **Your presence is a blessing forever.**

All: *Amen.*

238 All Saints'/All Souls Day litany

Today we remember all those saints who have gone before us. Their faithful lives and ideas form the foundation for our own lives of faith. They are people such as: St. Francis of Assisi, Hildegard von Bingen, Menno Simons, Conrad Grebel, George Fox, Daniel Kaufman, Mohatma Gandhi, Dr. Martin Luther King, Mother Teresa *(add your own names)*. We stand on the shoulders of their ideas, their faith, and their lives.

(silence)

Today we remember those whom we cannot name: the homeless, the abused, the refugees. Those who have perished as a result of the wars that dominated this year's news-papers—wars waged by our own nation, and wars waged by and within other countries.

(silence)

Today we remember those whose names we know very well, those close to us, those we touched and held, those we love.

(silence)

Our lives are a continual accumulation of memory, constantly growing, evolving, shifting, shrinking, at times slipping away entirely, at times catching us up with breathtaking force. Today we pause to carefully and thoughtfully tend to our memory of those who have gone before us. We remember, we pray, and we sing in order to close gaps in our own lives that will always remain open, to heal wounds that will always be tender, to tend our memories of those whose lives make each of us what we are today.

239 Prayer

Gracious God:
We remember those who have gone before us,
    whose lives have shaped our own,
      on whose shoulders we now stand.
Grant them rest, grant them peace.

We welcome those who come after us,
    whose lives we now shape,
    whose life foundations we now lay.
Grant them light, grant them peace.

Gracious God,
    grant us wisdom,
    grant us light,
    grant us rest,
    grant us peace. Amen.

Morning and Evening

Morning

240 Waiting in expectation

L: In the morning, O Lord,
      you hear my voice.
  In the morning I lay my requests before you
      and wait in expectation.

(Invite congregation to visualize requests in their open hands, and then to lift their hands, laying their requests before God. Wait in expectant silence.)

All: *In the morning, O Lord,*
      you hear my voice.
  In the morning I lay my requests before you
      and wait in expectation.

241 Logs and sawdust

Keep me mindful today, O God.
What offends me in others
    often resides in myself.

Remove the log in my own eye
    so I may neither blunder about
    nor cause pain and damage
    trying to eliminate specks of sawdust
    in the eye of my neighbor. Amen.

242 Awaken our souls

God of daybreak:
In the freshness of morning our souls awaken
    to the promptings of your Spirit.
Attune our ears to hear your voice
    calling us to a life of faith.
That we may say with Samuel:
    "Speak, Lord, for your servant is listening." Amen.

243 Default setting

Let your loving kindness
    become my default setting today, God.
If I'm suddenly shaken,
    may kindness spill out of my pores. Amen.

244 Cautious thanksgiving

Great Creator, Optimist and Agitator,
    we approach you this morning with cautious thanksgiving,
    knowing that true gratitude musters action.
Yet still, we risk these simple thank-yous
    and offer them in trust.

We thank you:
>for intricate beauty that blossoms into reverence,
>for your wild, windy Spirit
>and its undiscriminating taste in neighbors,
>for ugly pain transformed into glorious new beginnings,
>for surprising revelation born of blessing.

We praise you for truthful poets
>who beckon us into the abyss of darkness,
>who call us to remember your eternal covenant,
>and who remind us of your welcoming womb of mercy
>that births assurance and courage.

Thank you that we are never more or less than yours.

Bolster our perseverance as we think and grow
>beyond the false havens of conformity.

Embolden our words and our walk.

May your song reverberate from our voices and actions
>as we join the cosmos in everlasting praise.

This we pray in hope and faith of your kingdom come. Amen.

245 Beyond ease or comfort

Let us trust in you today, dear God.
May we grow beyond hope of ease or comfort
to the faithful surrender of ourselves
through the power of Christ. Amen.

246 Unfailing love

(from Psalm 143:8)

Let the morning bring me word of your unfailing love,
>*(silent or spoken reflections of gratitude)*
>for I have put my trust in you.
>*(silent or spoken affirmations of faith)*

Show me the way I should go,
>   *(silent or spoken prayers for guidance)*
>   for to you I lift up my soul.
>   *(silent or spoken intercessions)*
> Amen.

247 For morning light and fresh beginnings

> Creating God,
>   for morning light and fresh beginnings, we give thanks.
> Comfort those who awaken today with heavy hearts.
> Bless those who struggle to make ends meet.
> Protect those in danger or distress.
> Inspire us with a longing to do your will in each moment.
> We pray in the name of the One who makes all things new.
> Amen.

Evening

248 God's wrinkled hands

> We take everything that our day has held,
>   the best and the worst,
>   and we pile it into your wrinkled, loving hands.
> We take everything that the world has held today,
>   the good and the bad,
>   and we heap it all into your lap, Grandmother God.
> Then we crawl up into your lap, too.
> And still there is room for us and the whole world.

249 Free of unnecessary fears

Bless us tonight, O God.
Keep us safe from evil
    and from danger, within and without,
    free of all unnecessary fears.
May we meet you in our dreams.
Wake us in the morning,
    refreshed and ready for a new day
    with you and each other.
In Christ's name. Amen.

250 Evening examen

At evening we pause to remember the gift of this day.
For what did I hope at daylight?
What did I fear?
How have I known God's love and grace today?
How have I resisted God?
What do I need to confess?
How did I fulfill my call in the world today?
How did I offer love? Refuse love?
What unopened gift of promise remains with me tonight?
What do I need to offer into God's care and keeping—
    for myself? for the world?

God of the night watch,
    as stillness descends upon the earth
    and day passes into darkness,
hold us and all you love in tender care;
protect us as we sleep;
refresh our bodies, minds, and spirits
    so we may rise to love and serve you tomorrow.
We rest in your mercy and trust you forever. Amen.

Blessings

251 For a challenge

(based on Micah 6:8)

The Lord has told you what is required:
do not back away from the challenges before you today,
    but go from this place with joy,
    doing justice,
    loving mercy,
    and walking humbly.
The God of grace will go with you.

252 For a ministry

Sara

[*Name*], you are a unique creation of God,
    made in God's image.
We affirm that you have been called by God.
Remember that you are just a jar of clay,
    but you hold the precious gift of our resurrection hope.
May you be strong like a tree
    planted by the stream, the living water of Christ.
May God bless you, [*name*].

253 Mealtime song

(can be sung to the tune of "God is great")

God is great and God is good,
Lord, we thank you for this food.
Father God and Christ the Son,
Holy Spirit, nurturing one,
Moth'ring God feeds everyone.

254 Mealtime prayer

We are thankful, bountiful God, for this gift of food.
Bless those who have touched it along the way:
   farmers and field hands,
   pickers and packers,
   truckers and cooks.
We receive the good fruit of their labor
   with gratitude and joy. Amen.

255 Solstice

May these dark winter days
   find you free of seasonal depression,
   rested and content in such a fallow season.
May the darkness of these near-solstice days
   be like the dark richness of the fertile earth,
   hiding seeds of new life,
   ready to grow in their season.

256 Birth of a child

Mothering God, Fathering God—
Thank you for this new child, [*name*].

Thank you for breathing life into her/him.
Thank you that you know this child's name
    and that it is written on your heart.

Parenting God, bless [*name*].
May this child know that she/he is precious
    and that you will never forget her/him.
May [*name*] grow in wisdom and love. Amen.

257 Parent/child dedication prayer

(with parent's permission, pastor lifts the baby high)

Here you are God,
    this is the best we have,
    this baby boy/girl,
    your gift to us.

We offer this child back to you
    and seek your blessing and care
    for him/her,
    for his/her parents,
    and for us all. Amen.

258 Parent/child dedication

(possible text for bulletin cover)

Where these tiny toes will go
    no one knows
    but God
    who meets our feet
    in wind
    and water
    in sound
    and silence—
the Rock on which we walk.

259 Parent/child dedication congregational response

[*Name*], you are new to us, but you are not new to God. From all eternity, God has known your name. Now so do we. We welcome you as the child of [*parents' names*] and we love you as part of our congregation. May you grow in wisdom and knowledge and love of God. Amen.

260 A prayer for all children

O Jesus, who gathered children in your lap:
Today we pray
> for the children of our church,
> the children of our city,
> the children of our world.

May they live
> without fear of guns and bombs,
> without hunger for food or hunger for love,
> without the shadow of violence.

May each day bring them
> enough hugs for a smile,
> enough friends for security,
> enough adults for guidance,
> enough love for faith to grow.

Empower us to work with you
> to shape a world of justice
> for all your children. Amen.

261 For foster parents

God's Spirit moves among us and calls us to be servants in the Kingdom of God. [*Names of foster parents*], you have heard God's call to serve as foster parents, to open your

home to children who need special love and care. May you
be given a deep love for these children. As your church
family, we will also nurture your foster children as we
teach them, care for them, and become their friends. May
our shared life and witness help make your task both joyful
and fruitful.

262 For backpacks

(to be used at the start of the school year)

Wise and wonderful God, we dedicate these backpacks
    and bless the students who carry them.
Accompany the students to school.
Strengthen their minds and their bodies.
As they grow in knowledge,
    may they discover the gifts and passions
    that you have entrusted to them.
May they learn kindness, creativity, and care.
Bless their classmates, their teachers,
    and their parents, we pray. Amen.

263 For graduates

(can also be used on other occasions of transition)

May God bless you in this season of transition
    and grant you wisdom to perceive the path of integrity.
May Christ befriend you
    and bring you relationships to feed your soul.
May the Spirit go before you and guard your future
    so that you might know mercy in trouble,
        blessings in the ordinary, and faith in all things. Amen.

264 Graduation

L: God, you have created us in your image,
with minds to think, hearts to yearn,
and hands to create.
We give you thanks.

P: **We give thanks for these graduates**
who have studied, learned, questioned, synthesized,
grown, and finished their work.
Bless [*names of graduates*].

Grads: *We give thanks for those who have supported,*
encouraged, loved, and put up with us.
Bless our teachers, our families and friends.

L: God, you have come to us in Christ
and accompany us by your Holy Spirit.
Guide us in the way of truth and life.

P: **Walk with these graduates. Grant them wisdom and**
courage, strength and patience, hope and grace.

Grads: *Guide us in all knowledge and truth.*
Sharpen our minds and soften our hearts.
Widen our vision and deepen our faith.
Guard us from all danger and keep us close to you.

All: *We entrust ourselves to you—*
our past and our future,
our memories and our dreams.
Bless and keep us, for Christ's sake we pray. Amen.

265 Commencement

(for a public or interfaith setting)

Spirit of love, we rise to this day,
full of gratitude for the gifts, skills, and disciplines
that have carried these graduates to this day.

We are thankful for those who taught them
    with care and passion.
We rise, Spirit of Love, in your presence.
We hear you speak through pioneers
    and crafters of justice, dignity and beauty,
    crafters of imagination and hope.
We hear you say, "Hear, O children of earth.
    Seek peace and pursue it."
The desire of those who seek right and good relationships
    is like thirst for water and hunger for food.
We rise with determination
    to respond to the work of justice.
We rise with delight in the beauty
    of earth, community, and solidarity among friends.
For each of these who graduate today
    and for those who brought and nurtured them here
    we say "thank you" and "blessings upon you"
    in this glad hour. Amen.

266 For a young person leaving for school

Jesus, our Teacher, today we lift up [*name*] to you
    and seek your blessing on him/her as he/she begins
    college/university.
As a youth, O Lord, you went to the temple to study.
As an adult you taught others by words and actions
    in the temple, in the meadows, on the mountains and seas.
May [*name*]'s instructors teach with respect
    and honor the educational task they have been given.
As [*name*] begins his/her studies, may he/she increase
    in knowledge, wisdom, and understanding—
    of you and your creation,
    and of the subject matter he/she pursues.

Grant rest after late nights of study,
>moments of fun to accompany the times of work,
>and plenty of joy and friendship when he/she is homesick.

May [*name*] always know that you are walking with him/her.
We ask this in the name of the One
>who walks with us and teaches us all. Amen.

267 For a young adult

L: Young adulthood is a time of endings and beginnings.

1: You are making a transition from the time
>when we called you a child or a teen.

2: You are no longer a helpless infant, a dependent child,
or a teenager in the first throes of independence.

L: As a church, we recognize and celebrate
>your many accomplishments in life so far.

1: You have studied and learned much.

2: You have been introduced to the world of work
>at home and at your jobs.

1: You have learned to make friendships and cherish them.

2: You have made important decisions about your faith.

L: Now you are saying "hello" to adulthood,
>where much will be expected of you.

1: You leave behind the security
>of others making your decisions for you.

2: You decide for yourselves
>how to use your time, money and energy.

1: You decide where to live, how to live,
>with whom you will live, and for whom you will live.

2: You decide how to claim the faith
>that others have taught and modeled for you.

All: *As a church, we welcome you to this scary, exciting,*
and challenging world of adulthood.

We offer you our support and love
  for the years of discovery that lie ahead.
We challenge you to remember God, who offers help
  to you and to all of us on this journey of life.

268 Wedding

[*Name*] and [*name*], may you always dwell
  in the love of your Creator.
May Christ weave you into a tapestry of hope.
May the Spirit build you into a house of good will.
May your sorrows be halved and your joys be doubled.
May your nights be restful and your days adventurous.
May you have many years together,
  growing wise and full of the knowledge of God.
May all who are here go out
  renewed in life, light, and holiness.
In the name of God our Creator, Christ our Savior,
  and the Spirit who dwells among us. Amen.

269 Wedding call and blessing

We are gathered here
  as family and friends of [*name*] and [*name*]
  to witness ancient and sacred promises,
  which will be spoken in our hearing.

For some, it is a reminder of the day
  when we, too, made such vows.
For others it may awaken aspiration and hope.
But for all of us,
  we meet in the midst of a mystery of rare beauty,
  a divine mystery!

Let us, then, prepare ourselves
in a moment of silence.
(silence)

Ancient of Days, Fountain of life and love:
We have come to seek for [*name*] and [*name*]
that blessing beyond human power to give,
that blessing which only you can grant.
Be near to them now
as they mark this beginning with solemn vows.
Give them strength to hold these promises,
so they, and we who are gathered,
may come to reflect your steadfastness,
your loyalty, your abiding tenderness and love.
In such gifts as these we aspire to establish our homes
and in those places be joyfully content.
For love of your only Son our Savior, we pray. Amen.

270 Wedding

May our Creator God of Adam and Eve,
    bless your marriage with grace and forgiveness.
May our Covenant God of Sarah and Abraham,
    bless your marriage with laughter and surprise.
May our Providing God of Ruth and Boaz,
    bless your marriage with compassion and friendship.
May our Passionate God of Solomon's love songs
    bless your marriage with excitement and wonder.
May our Savior God of Joseph and Mary,
    bless your marriage with promise and hope.
And may our Redeeming God of Christ and the Church,
    bless your marriage with the depths of love
        and the mysteries of joy! Amen.

271 **For a golden wedding anniversary**

Now may the God who has faithfully walked with you
through these past fifty years
guide and protect you through the years ahead.
May God grant you strength and wisdom, courage and grace
to face the challenges of aging
and the joys of retirement.
May you continue to serve,
sharing your wisdom and experience,
loving the next generation,
and deepening your love for one another
as long as you both shall live. Amen.

272 **For marriages**

*Lines can be reassigned for up to eight couples. They can also be
personalized to the couples' experience.*

Pastor: Gracious God, you make light to shine
over the earth and all its inhabitants.
You renew the earth with rain and snow;
daily you continue your work of creation,
as you bring harmony and sustenance to nature
and peace to our lives.
People: **Today we give thanks for the mysterious way
you create and sustain marriages.
We marvel at the intricate way two lives
can be woven together in caring, loyalty, and trust.**
Couples: *We thank you for simple pleasures of married life:*
Couple 1: for the safe feeling of at-home-ness with another;
Couple 2: for the gestures that help us know we're cared for;
Couple 3: for the delights of married love;
Couple 4: for the wonder of another person who knows us
better than anyone else and likes us anyway.

Couples:	*We also bring the dark moments of our lives:*
Couple 1:	when we hurt our partner, knowingly or not;
Couple 2:	when we treat the other person with disrespect;
Couple 3:	when we don't know what to do with our anger;
Couple 4:	when we want to stifle the other person's growth for our own advantage.
Couples:	*For these failures, we ask your forgiveness, merciful God.*
People:	**Today we seek your sustaining grace for the growth of these marriages.**
Couples:	*May our love be refined in the crucible of life, when we are tested by disappointment or become acquainted with grief. Wrap us in patience when crises threaten us, and protect our marriage bonds from harm. Lead us toward mature love, sustained by your own love for us, which is beyond measure.*
All:	**As each season in nature offers its own beauty, may each season of marriage express the beauty of God's love. May God give grace and courage for what is yet to come. Amen.**

273 Pet blessing

God of all creation,
>   we bring to you our companions, our pets.
The love you have for your creation
>   is reflected in these animals.
Thank you for their form, color, texture, motion—
>   all your work of art;
>   may we grow in appreciation of your masterful creation.
Thank you for the pleasure, playfulness, and humor
>   that our pets display;
>   may we learn such joy from them.

Thank you for their friendship, especially when we're lonely;
  may we learn such companionship from them.
Thank you for our pets' wisdom, innocence, loyalty
  and unqualified acceptance;
    may we learn such loyalty from them.
Bless our animal friends with good health,
  happy lives, and protection from harm.
Heal the sick, protect those who are lost,
  and guide them to safety.
Thank you for your gift of love
  offered to us through these pets. Amen.

274 Pet blessing

God, you created our pets
  and said, "These are good."
You created Adam and Eve,
  and asked them to name the animals.
So now we name these pets that we bring before you.
  (pet owners name their animals)
Bless these friends and companions,
  and make them a blessing to others.
May they bring joy and laughter where there are tears,
  comfort and healing where there is loneliness.
And may we as caregivers learn a lesson
  from the unconditional love and loyalty they share.
Teach us to trust you, as our animals trust us. Amen.

Laments

275 No words to speak

(appropriate after a great tragedy)

L: When there are no words to speak healing into our hurt,
P: we gather together in the sound of sheer silence.
L: When we feel inadequate to come into the Presence,
P: we grovel at the foot of the Savior.
L: When we don't even have the energy to pray,
P: we rely on the Spirit to cry out on our behalf.
All: *Lord, hear our cry. Amen.*

276 Untimely death

Eternal, compassionate God, our hearts are heavy with grief
    as we struggle with the death in our community.
We need your help.
Surround us with the warmth and strength of your embrace.
Speak your comfort above all the questions and confusion
    swirling in our heads.
Touch our eyes, blurry with sadness and fatigue,
        that we might catch sight of your radiant and unfailing
            love.
God of all time and consolation,
    help us to worship you this day.
We ask these things in Jesus' name. Amen.

277 In times of heightened fear and anxiety

(based on Isaiah 43)

L: Hear the word of the Lord:
    "Fear not, for I have saved you;
        I have called you by name; you are mine."

P: **God our Savior, we confess our fear,**
        which keeps us from fully loving our neighbors,
        our enemies, and even you.
    Call us by name and save us!
    (silence)

L: "When you pass through the waters, I will be with you;
        and when you pass through the rivers,
        they will not drown you."

P: **God our Keeper, the waters are getting higher.**
    Our jobs, families, finances, and responsibilities
        overwhelm us.
    The troubles of the world exhaust us.
    We lift the sinful worry of these chaotic waters to you.
    Pull us to dry land!
    (silence)

L: "When you walk through the fire, you will not be burned;
        the flames will not set you ablaze."

P: **God our Protector, we confess**
        that we do not always fully trust you.
    Instead, we trust our politics, our technology,
        our entertainment, more than you.
    Forgive our idolatry.
    (silence)

L: "Do not be afraid, for I the Lord God, am with you.
    I love you. You are precious in my sight." Amen.

278 Call to worship

(based on Psalm 137)

L: Come, let us worship God, who laughs and cries with us.
   Let us praise the One whose suffering
        encompasses the breadth of our pain,
        and whose delight surpasses our deepest joy.
**P: We worship the God who knows our thoughts and
        feelings even before we name them.**
   **We honor the One who welcomes our laments
        as well as our songs of thanksgiving.**
All: *May all the words of our mouths
        and the meditations of our hearts
        be acceptable in your sight, O God. Amen.*

279 Raging hearts prayer

(based on Psalm 137)

O, God, by the river of [*a local river*], we sit and weep,
        remembering with longing the glorious days of the past.
Sometimes we are so overcome with grief that we cannot sing.
   How can we sing when so much change
        makes what was once familiar seem so foreign to us?
        (silence)
If you are the God of steadfast love, then why so much change?
   Why so much loneliness?
   Why so much neediness, O God?
        (silence)
Save us, for we pour out our anger and fears before you.
Better our raging hearts open before you,
        than hearts of stone hidden behind forced smiles.
Hear our cries, and turn our pain into joy.

Do not dash our dreams against a rock,
>   but carry us through the journey of death,
>   the pain of labor,
>   to the delight of birth.
We lift our cry to you
>   in the name of your Son Jesus, the Christ. Amen.

280 For our city

(based on Psalm 137; adapt to local realities)

L: By the waters of the [*name*] River, we sit down and weep,
>   for the victims of another school shooting,
>   for the loss of our children's innocence.
   From the depths of our sin and sadness we cry out to you:
P: Lord, hear our prayer.
L: By the waters of the [*name*] River we sit down and weep,
>   at the horror of famine, AIDS, and drought,
>   for a tragedy so immense we cannot comprehend it,
>   for lives and crops that are lost,
>   for orphans and hunger that multiply.
   From the depths of our sin and sadness we cry out to you:
P: Lord, hear our prayer.
L: By the waters of the [*name*] River we sit down and weep,
>   for the consumerism that erodes our souls
>   for the entertainment industry that mocks your values
>   for our hearts, broken by addiction, depression,
>   and uncertain health.
   From the depths of our sin and sadness we cry out to you:
P: Be not deaf to our poor pleading,
Lord in your mercy, hear our prayer. Amen.

281 Gathering for a service of lament

L: In our weakest moments, through the darkest hours,
P: you walk with us.

L: In our moments of joy, through the brightest celebrations,
P: you walk with us.
L: In our abundance,
P: you walk with us.
L: In our poverty,
P: you walk with us.
L: To the cross,
P: you walk with us.
L: Even through death,
P: you walk with us.
L: Into new abundant life,
P: you walk with us.
L: Because we cannot do it alone,
P: you walk with us.
L: Lord, grant us grace to follow. Amen.

282 We wait in hope

(based on Psalm 130)

From the depths of our sadness
    we cry out to you, merciful God:
    hear us,
    heal us,
    strengthen us.
Show us how to be your people.
Teach us to walk in your ways, without fear.
Encourage us to build bridges and not walls,
    to risk our lives for your reign.

Rock our complacency, mighty God.
Give us a vision of the New Jerusalem.
For you have surely walked with us in the past.
You have taught us and carried us to this place.

Therefore we sing of your love and mercy,
    your justice and your shalom.
We proclaim your goodness as we wait in hope
        for your love to cast out fear
        and change our lives.

Then we will sing of your praises
    by the riverbanks of our city.
Then we will acknowledge that you alone are God
    forever and ever. Amen.

283 Prayer for a family in crisis
(when a child has run away; adapt to local setting)

Compassionate God, we are afraid.
We fear for the safety of [*name*].
Wrap your arms of protection around him/her.
Keep him/her safe from physical danger and evil influences.
Guide [*name*] to a safe place until he/she returns home.
And when he/she returns, make us wise
        in seeking reconciliation.

Comforting God, be a shelter to [*names of child and parents*]
        during this storm.
Make their home a place where [*name*] can feel loved and safe,
        and where [*parents' names*] can feel trusted and respected.
Remind them often that you walk with each of them.
May your peace fill them today and in the days ahead.
May your wisdom guide them.
We pray in the name of Jesus who knows our anguish. Amen.

284 For natural disasters

After a tragedy, words are inadequate. Worshippers should be oriented to the silence and meditation that is at the heart of this prayer.

You have kept count of our tossings, O Lord,
    you have put our tears in your bottle.
Are they not in your record?
(Moments of silence. Then invite worshippers to imagine God kneeling beside their beds at night, catching their tears and making notes about their suffering.)

Today when we call, this we know:
    that God is for us.
(Moments of silence. Then invite worshippers to consider how God has been present for them in the past despite their current loss and pain.)

In God, whose word we praise,
    in the Lord, whose name we honor,
    in God we trust; we are not afraid. Amen.
(Free spoken prayers. Then invite worshippers to reaffirm confidence and trust in God.)

285 Prayer for a church in the midst of a dilemma

God of light and truth, Holy Spirit of wisdom and guidance,
    we call upon you in the midst of our confusion.
As we struggle to understand your will amid our dilemma,
    we still seek your light.

Grant us truth that will set us free,
    even from our own self-righteousness.

Guide our discernment
>   so we may attain your wisdom and justice. Strengthen
>   the bond of your love
>   so we may seek the good of others.

Wipe away the hurt we have caused and the hurt we have felt.
Restore us in your love; we cry to you.

Now, as we make our decision, lead us by your Holy Spirit.
Enlighten our eyes
>   so we may achieve your good and perfect will.
And in doing so, may we rejoice in you.
We ask this in the name of our Lord Jesus. Amen.

286 More is expected of us

(based on Matthew 5:43-48)

L: God's faithful gather from the world—but are not of it.

P: We are God's people. Can we claim it?

L: The world says, "Love your neighbor and hate your
>   enemy."

P: We are God's people. Can we claim it?

L: The world reserves love for friends who think alike.

P: We are God's people. Can we claim it?

L: The world honors deception, shrewd deals, and lies.

P: We are God's people. Can we claim it?

L: The world justifies revenge and "getting even."

P: We are God's people. Can we claim it?

L: The world returns insult with insult.

P: We are God's people. Can we claim it?

L: The world is quick to label some
>   as "lazy," "ignorant," "worthless."

P: We are God's people. Can we claim it?

L: We come from our world to worship
>   and to be reminded of who we are.

All: *Let us open our hearts and lives*
to God's transforming power.
May God be praised in our worship. Amen.

287 For a divorce

P: Dear [*name*], our hearts grieve for you. We, too, feel the disappointments and hurts in the ending of your marriage. Something that held so much hope at one point in your life has come to such a sad end. We accept your remorse and extend to you our forgiveness and love— both now and in the future. May our solidarity offer you strength in the days ahead.

Prayer

L: Merciful God, we bring our prayers to you for [*name*],
who has suffered the death of his/her marriage,
May he/she know your healing
and accept the gift of new life.
Bless him/her with freedom and peace.

P: **Lord, hear our prayer.**

L: For [*names of children*], that they may continue to know
the love of their parents
and above all, your love, O God.
May they share in the gift of new life.

P: **Lord, hear our prayer.**

L: For those people, some present and some absent,
who have supported this marriage in the past
and now undertake to support new life—

P: **Lord, hear our prayer.**

L: For those who are not reconciled to this separation,
bring healing and peace.

P: **Lord, hear our prayer.**

L: For the anxieties of an unknown future,
may we all put our trust in you.

P: Lord, hear our prayer.

L: For the grace to assume new responsibilities,
        that we may serve you and love others—

P: Lord, hear our prayer.

L: Accept the prayers of your people, loving God.
     Look with compassion upon us
        and all who turn to you for help.
     To you we give glory, praise and thanks,
        now and forever. Amen.

Dedications

288 Dedication of Bibles for children

Leader 1: [*Names*], we give you these Bibles
as gifts from our congregation.
Children, tell us: How will you hear God's Word?

Children: With our ears.

Leader 2: How will you touch God's Word?

Children: With our hands.

Leader 1: How will you smell God's Word?

Children: With our noses.

Leader 2: How will you see God's Word?

Children: With our eyes.

Leader 1: How will you taste God's Word?

Children: With our tongues.

Leader 2: How will you follow God's Word?

Children: With our whole lives.

Leader 1: May we all be students of the Bible
as we study and worship together.

289 Dedication of Bibles for adults
(adapt as antiphonal reading at dedication of pew Bibles)

**P: In the beginning was the Word, and the Word
was with God
and the Word was God.**

L: The Word shines with the constancy of a star,
>   leading the slave to freedom.
>   It illuminates with its beam
>   the corridors of ignorance and fear.
>   It dances with delicate feet
>   across the sluices of sorrow.
>   It warms even the grave with its eternal flame of truth.

P: **All those who love the Word,**
>   **be as fearless daredevils who swallow the flame**
>   **so that it may dwell within them!**

Recipients: *We come as searchers of truth, desiring that*
>   *God's Word blaze in our hearts.*

L: Come, fellow pilgrims, join us
>   as we carry our lanterns into the bowels of the
>   earth.
>   or as we bask on the sunlit hills of Galilee.

P: **Let the Scriptures take you on a journey of faith**
>   **that leads inward and outward.**

Recipients: *The light of God's Word will be a lamp to our feet.*

L: Beloved of God, cherish the Word.
>   It will sustain you when all else fails.

All: *May the Word illumine the pathways we walk*
>   *and bring us home at the end. Amen.*

290 House blessing

(each room blessing may be given by a different person)

Peace be to this house and to all who dwell in it.
>   *(walk together into living area)*
God, our dwelling place, send your blessing to everyone
who visits here. May they be knit together in fellowship
and renewed in their spirits.
>   *(walk together into kitchen/dining room)*
God, our provider, you fill the hungry with good things.
Bless those who work in this kitchen. May all who eat here

give their thanksgiving for daily bread, grateful for your
mercy and mindful of others' needs.

(walk together to the bedrooms and repeat for each one)
God, our keeper, you watch over us when we are awake and
when we sleep. Grant peaceful rest to those who enter here.

(look out together over neighborhood)
God of all, we commend this neighborhood to your care.
May it be set free from social strife and decay and stand as
a community of peace.

(walk back to an entryway or where group began)
God of creation, bless the inhabitants of this house with
freedom and joy. Visit them with your love. Be near to them
in times of struggle, and preserve us all in your peace. Amen.

291 Blessing for a vehicle

(adapt for a family or work trip)

Lord, please bless this vehicle.
Protect me from other drivers
    and protect others from me.
Guide me to drive wisely
    and to look for ways to drive less,
    for the sake of your planet,
    and our own well-being. Amen.

292 Blessing for a bicycle

Bless my bike, dear God,
    and bless my feet, too.
May I ride in the clear air of your Spirit
    and meet you at every turn. Amen.

293 Blessing for a workplace

(co-workers could join in this prayer)

Laboring God,
I spend so much of my life at work.
Bless this time and space.
May my efforts honor you, my colleagues, and the
     common good.
Make me a peaceable and patient advocate for your values
     here—
    in my interactions with others,
    in my decisions and quality of work,
    in my use of resources and power.
Bless the work of this organization
     so we may contribute to your justice and healing
     in this hurting world. Amen.

294 Ground-breaking for a church building

(can be used with Psalm 84:1-4)

Pastor: To the glory of God, we act together
           to break ground for our new church facility.
           The responsibility and the privilege rest upon us all
           to build a house of worship to our Lord,
           and a center for service to our community.
Child: We are building a church here
           where children can learn to love God,
           and grow in grace and goodness.
           (a child digs)
Youth: We are building a church here
           where youth can be challenged to claim our future,
           and prepare to serve in the name of Christ.
           (a youth digs)

Adult: We are building a church here
        where we can worship and fellowship
        and build together a community of hope
            and peace.
        (an adult digs)

Senior: We are building a church here
        where we can claim inner peace
        found in Christ, who has brought us thus far.
        (a senior adult digs)

Building
 chair: We are building a church here
        to express with our gifts and our labor
        the vision we have been given.
        We will build it together for God's mission on earth.
        (building chair digs)

Architect: We are building a church here
        with our very best in craft and workmanship.
        We construct this building for your praise.
        (architect digs)

Pastor: With great joy we instruct the work to begin.
        With God's grace and direction,
        we are building a church here, together. Amen.

295 Ground-breaking for a church building

This prayer can be used with "What is this place" (HWB 1)
and 1 Corinthians 3:9-11 and 1 Peter 2:4-10.

1:   We praise you, living God,
        for the joy we find in the church;
        for communion with each other;
        for generosity and spiritual nurture;
        for visible expressions of holiness in our midst.
P: **Lead us in your ways through your church.**

2: We give you thanks
for the vision that came to dwell on this ground;
the laborers who prepared us for this time;
the service of today's leaders
who point the direction for tomorrow's church.

P: **Make us ever mindful of each person's contribution
to the life of your church.**

3: We are grateful for the eye of the planner,
the tempered patience of the crafter and engineer,
the calloused hands of the builders
who all labor for our common good.

P: **Let no talent be overlooked in the building of your reign
and let us never fail to acknowledge
each offering made to your church.**

4: We call to you, O God, to pour out your spirit among us.
May we be builders of a holy temple,
where people find peace in the face of turmoil.
May we be servants and visionaries,
planters and harvesters,
stewards of a living treasure.

P: **May the church we build be strong and beautiful,
a testimony of your grace,
May the body of Christ thrive in this place.
May the world see an increase of your love,
justice and peace. Amen.**

296 For a new building

*(based on Psalm 18:2, Matthew 7:25, Ephesians 2:21-22,
1 Corinthians 3:11, 1 Peter 2:4-5)*

1: God is my rock, my fortress and deliverer.
2: God is my rock, in whom I take refuge.
1&2: God is my rock.
3: Rocks,
2&3: stones,

1-3:   and bricks

2:   have been cemented together to create this building.

3:   Rocks,

2&3:   stones,

1-3:   and bricks,

1:   laid on a strong foundation.

3:   Those who hear my words and put them into practice are like a person building a house, who dug down deep and laid the foundation on rock. When the flood came, the torrent struck that house but could not shake it, because it was well built.

No one can lay any foundation other than the one already laid, which is Jesus Christ.

2:   Rocks,

2&3:   stones,

1-3:   and bricks,

2:   laid on a strong foundation.

1:   In Jesus the whole building is joined together and rises to become a holy temple in the Lord. And in Jesus, you too are being built together to become a building in which God lives by the Spirit.

3:   Like living stones may we be built into a spiritual house, to be a holy priesthood, to offer spiritual sacrifices acceptable to God through Jesus Christ.

2:   Rocks,

2&3:   stones,

1-3:   and bricks,

2:   laid on a strong foundation.

Commissioning and releasing

297 For pastoral caregivers

Our loving God, we thank you for placing us in a community
of care, where we can weep with those who cry and rejoice
with those who laugh. We thank you for those who offer
special gifts of care on our behalf—at a hospital bedside, in
a nursing home, among the aged, with everyone who makes
important transitions.

For these caregivers we pray:
    sensitivity to the broad range
        of human concerns they will encounter;
    calm in the face of tragedy and loss;
    contagious hope nourished by your Spirit;
    recall of Scriptures or hymns to offer as encouragement;
    grace for the unexpected;
    wisdom when they feel unprepared;
    joy and fulfillment as they go about their ministries
        in our congregation and community.

Make us receptive to their care. Open our eyes to see the
living Christ in these caregivers. In the name of Jesus, the
Good Shepherd who calls each of us by name. Amen.

298 Prayer of the pastor upon installation

(based on Psalm 61)

Hear my cry, O God; listen to my prayer.
From the end of the earth I call to you
    when my heart is faint.
Lead me to the rock that is higher than I;
    for you are my refuge, a strong tower against the enemy.
Let me abide in your tent forever,
    find refuge under the shelter of your wings.
For you, O God, have heard my vows;
    you have given me the heritage of those who fear your
        name.
As I keep my vows day after day,
    I will always sing praises to your name. Amen.

299 For the installation of a pastor

(children and others may gesture at italicized words)

God, bless [*name*]'s *heart.*
Give him/her your indwelling spirit ,
    calling him/her to love you and to live anchored to Christ.
God, bless [*name*]'s *eyes.*
Give him/her your wisdom, teaching him/her to perceive
      your desires
    and to see your vision of compassion.
God, bless [*name*]'s *hands.*
Give him/her your faith and trust, binding his/her hand
      to this team of leaders, to this body,
    and to all those he/she will serve in faith, love and hope.
God, bless [*name*]'s *feet.*
Give him/her the gospel of peace,
    guiding him/her to lead the congregation in your ways.
God, bless this congregation whom [*name*] now serves
    as a member and as a pastor.

300 For the ordination of a pastor

(each paragraph can be read by a different leader)

Holy God, we thank you for the women and men you have called to your service in every part of the globe. We rejoice in the discernment that has brought [*name*] to this time and place. We give special thanks for his/her sense of call and his/her capacity for pastoral leadership.

Release in [*name*] all the gifts needed for the ministries to which he/she has been called. Use his/her gifts of communication to passionately proclaim the good news of your love; his/her organizational gifts to broaden this church's mission; his/her pastoral gifts to offer joy and hope to others; his/her theological insights to enrich and expand the vision and identity of this congregation.

Protect [*name*] from impulsiveness, when good ideas come faster than the church can accommodate them; from cynicism when things move too slowly or contrary to his/her best judgment; from shallowness when he/she faces too much to do in too little time; and from self-doubt when criticism comes his/her way. Give him/her all the resources needed for a long and effective ministry as he/she grows toward full maturity in Christ.

Provide [*name*] with a strong network of support and a trusting partnership with his/her pastoral colleagues. Bless the members and leaders of this congregation with a genuine openness to be nurtured and stretched by his/her presence among them.

In the name of Jesus, the foundation and cornerstone of the church, where we are all united as living stones into one new creation, Amen.

301 For a pastor's sabbatical leave

Leader: As Jesus withdrew from the crowds to be renewed before God for ministry, so you too enter a time of reflection, study, prayer, and renewal. As a congregation we recognize this time apart as an expression of your call to serve the people of God.

Deacons/Elders: We affirm your preparation for this sabbatical, and we share your vision for personal and congregational renewal. We will walk with you in your leaving, in your time away, and in your returning.

Pastor: I am thankful to God and the congregation for the gift of this sabbatical. I will use the time wisely, in order to fulfill the goals I have set for myself. I will miss you while I am away, and I look forward to returning for further ministry among you. May God watch over us while we are absent from each other.

Congregation: We commission you to accept this time as a gift of God for the renewal of your calling. We commit you and your family to God's loving care while you are away. We commit ourselves to respect your separation from us. We commit ourselves to activate the spiritual gifts among us, thus making this a time of self-discovery and growth for us as well as for you.

We look forward to your renewed ministry among us, and to the continued growth of this congregation's ministry to each other and to the world. In the name of Christ, Amen.

(302) Sabbatical blessing

(can be voiced by one or several congregational leaders)

Take a long, deep breath.
Change the rhythm of your days.
Open your interior space,
    leaving behind the clutter of endless responsibilities,
    weekly deadlines of worship,
    unfinished lists of to-dos.
Savor that open space.
May it be filled with the delightful presence
    of the One who says, "Come away and rest awhile."
In your sabbatical may you find
    new energy and passion,
    deep insight and understanding,
    and fresh Spirit-leading for your journey.
And in your returning may you lead us again,
    renewed by the blessing of your time away.

303 Blessing and release for departing pastor

(adapt to local circumstances)

1: We have laughed and cried,
    worshipped and prayed together.
2: Together we have hoped, dreamed, worked, and eaten
    potlucks.
P: Now it is time to say goodbye.
1: Parting is bittersweet. Memories flood our minds
    and hearts.
**P: We say goodbye with gratitude and sadness mixed
together.**
2: In saying goodbye to [*name*], we release him/her from
    responsibilities as pastor at [*name of church*]. Will you
    join me in this release?

P: With God's help, we release [*name*] from his/her responsibilities as our pastor.

Pastor: As a symbol of this release, I give to you, [*name of congregational chair*], a new pair of glasses. I pray that under your leadership as chair, this congregation will keep on living out God's vision, sensitive to where God's Spirit wishes to lead you.

P: With God's help, we will keep on living out God's vision for us.

Pastor: And to you, [*name of pastoral committee chair*], I give my hospital visiting card. I pray that under your leadership in pastoral care, this congregation will keep on caring for one another, in familiar ways, and in ways yet to be imagined.

P: With God's help, we will keep on caring.

Pastor: And to you, [*name of worship committee chair*], I give a copy of the hymnal in which we keep track of the hymns we sing each Sunday. I pray that under your leadership of the worship committee, this congregation will keep on worshipping God, combining old and new expressions in vital, authentic ways.

P: With God's help, we will keep on worshipping God in ways that are authentic for us.

Pastor: To you, [*name of the stewardship committee chair*], I give my keys to the church and to my office, recognizing that this will no longer be the setting in which I minister.

P: With God's help, we release you, [*name*], as our pastor.

1: As we release [*name*] from ministry in our congregation, we also ask God's blessing on his/her future ministry.

P: **We offer support and encouragement to you, [name], as your ministry unfolds in new settings. We pray God's blessings on you and on us as we begin a new relationship with each other, in which you are no longer our pastor.**

2: Now I ask you, [name], do you release this congregation from its loyalty to you as a pastor? Do you release its members from turning to you and depending on you to provide the pastoral ministries they seek?

Pastor: I do, with the help of God. I pray God's blessing on each person's spiritual journey, and I pray God's blessing on [name of congregation] in its continued ministry.

(if team setting)
To you, [name of second pastor], I give this baptismal pitcher, which belonged to this congregation long before either one of us began here as a pastor. I pray God's blessing on you and your future colleagues in ministry as you lead this church community.

1: Let us join in prayer.

All: *Eternal God, you have been our refuge and strength through the years of our life together. Give us a strong sense of your presence as we now go our separate ways. Enlarge our faith, that we may see your unfolding purpose in this time. Be our guide through dark and doubt. Grant us peace in doing your will. Bless us as we move into your future. In Jesus' name we pray. Amen.*

304 For Christian Education Sunday

(adapted from Deuteronomy 6, Psalms 78)

1: The Lord is our God, the Lord alone.
2: We will love the Lord our God with all our heart, all our soul, all our mind.

3: We will keep God's word in our heart.

4: The Word of the Lord will be recited to the children,
and to the youth, and to the adults.

1: We will remind and encourage one another
to study God's Word.

2: We will share with each other
how God has walked with us on our journey.

3: We will kindle the faith of the congregation
with words of affirmation, challenge, and love.

4: We are God's work of art—each one of us!

1: Like stained glass we will let God's love shine through us
reflecting the good news of Jesus Christ.

2: Together we will let the Holy Spirit use our lives
to proclaim God's story.

3: Together we will listen and become quiet before God.

1-4: Together we will tell of all God's wonderful
and glorious deeds.

305 For Sunday school teachers

(can be used mid-year to encourage and sustain teachers)

L: God of wisdom, today we recognize the gift of teaching
in our community of faith:
For [*name*] and [*name*] who have the patience to work
with our nursery class, who make those first positive
impressions of Sunday school,

P: **we give you thanks.**

L: For [*name*] and [*name*] who foster curiosity about God
and answer the endless questions of our preschoolers,

P: **we give you thanks.**

L: For [*name*] and [*name*] who encourage our primary
children to love God and each other,

P: **we give you thanks.**

L: For [*name*] and [*name*] who harness the energy of our
middlers into exploring the Bible,

P: **we give you thanks.**

L: For [*name*] and [*name*] who absorb the ups and downs of our junior youth and point them to Jesus,

P: **we give you thanks.**

L: For [*name*] and [*name*] who nudge our youth to explore how God can be involved in each part of their lives,

P: **we give you thanks.**

L: For our teachers of adults [*names*] who challenge their peers to live faithfully,

P: **we give you thanks.**

L: We have called out those with gifts for teaching, O God. We are grateful for their commitment to you and to us. Grant them strength, hope and joy in serving. Fill them with wisdom, love and the power of your Spirit as they carry out the church's ministries of nurture and education. Amen.

306 For church ministries

1: Our Loving God calls us, as the church, to reflect Christ's light to each other and to the world, in the power of the Spirit.

2: Today we dedicate to you, O God, the gifts we offer through the work of this congregation.

1: God calls us to ministries of spiritual formation and pastoral care.

2: Patient and compassionate God, bless the ways we offer support in times of suffering and loss. Strengthen our relationships as we hold each other accountable to our Christian witness. Bless our fellowship. And may our study and conversation encourage spiritual growth in our homes and congregational ministries.

P: We dedicate to God our ministries of spiritual formation, pastoral care, and community life. May we be a light of Christ in the world.

1: God calls us to ministries of witness and reconciliation, locally and globally.

2: Just and merciful God, challenge our complacency, and bless our work for justice in the world. Enrich our relationships as parents, children, sisters, brothers, spouses, grandparents, grandchildren, friends, colleagues, and neighbors. May our workplaces and homes be locations of faithful witness.

P: We dedicate to God our ministries of witness and reconciliation. May we be a peacemaking community; a light of Christ in the world.

1: God has given us the ministry of the Sabbath.

2: God of Jubilee, bless our preparation and participation in liturgies of praise, confession, and thanksgiving. Uphold those who encourage us to greater stewardship of time, talent, and tithe. May the ways we administer our financial giving be a sign of faithful Sabbath-sharing to those in need.

P: We dedicate our ministries of Sabbath-keeping. May we honor God in worship and rest, trusting that God will multiply our offerings.

All: *In all things, may we be lights for you in this world. Amen.*

307 Recognition and release of a lay leader

P: Thank you, God, for the gift of [name]. In his/her ministry, we see your love, truth, and grace. Because of [name]'s example and gentle nudging, you have become more real to us. You are present in [*name*]'s encouraging words, sensitive listening, thoughtful counsel, and warm and comforting presence. Forgive us for times when we were ungrateful or unsupportive.

Bless [*name*] as he/she leaves this assignment and serves in other ways. Bless us as we follow you under new leadership. We seek your Spirit's guidance and power. Amen.

L: Because [*name*]'s leadership and ministry have been significant to him/her and to us, the end of this assignment requires us to make important adjustments in our relationships. [*Name*] will be giving up the privileges and the responsibilities that go with lay ministry. He/she may feel both relief and loss. It may take time for him/her and for us to adjust to our new relationship. We commit ourselves to make this necessary transition comfortable and complete.

P: [*Name*], we release you from the responsibilities we asked you to carry when you were called to this ministry. We pledge our continuing support and friendship. We know you will no longer be available to us in the same capacity. We invite you to help us relate to you in new ways.

Lay leader: As I once welcomed the call to serve you, I now also welcome your release from that call. Though I will no longer be one of your ministers, I intend to serve the church in other ways. I pledge my support to those who continue or who will begin to lead this congregation. Please help me relate to you in new ways.

L: In the church, we take turns serving and being served. Let us join in expressing our commitment to service by singing together "Will you let me be your servant" (HWB 307).

Special Services

308 The Longest Night: Light in our darkness

Visuals: In various ways our sanctuaries in December will already reflect the themes of the Advent and Christmas season. For this service consider adding only these simple elements on the communion table, or on an additional table at the front of the sanctuary: One tall glass cylinder filled with water and a large floating candle. Surrounding this add several wide, clear glass bowls, filled with water. On the table, scatter additional small floating candles that will be used later in the service. Consider leaving the lighting in the sanctuary low, though bright enough to read bulletins and hymnals.

Words for meditation   **Psalm 28:1-2**

Music for gathering
Consider simple, reflective instrumental music to set a contemplative tone.

Welcome
For those who dwell in the Northern Hemisphere the proclamations of Advent and Christmas are heard when the days are short and the nights long. It is a poignant time of year to proclaim the coming of the Light that will not be overcome by any darkness. Tonight, on the longest night of the year, we remember this promise and we acknowledge the darkness of grief and loss in our lives that longs for this Light. Here we honor the presence of those for whom there may be sadness rather than "tidings of good cheer" as Christmas approaches. It is for ones such as these that the Christ child comes.

A call to worship
Center floating candle is lit during the reading.

L: We gather as day turns to memory
and night is drawn across the land.
**P: You are the light of the world;
be a light in our darkness, O Christ.**
L: The dark of night can seem pale
to one whose life is shrouded by sorrow.
**P: You are the light of the world;
be a light in our darkness, O Christ.**
L: Where do we go when our eyes cannot see you?
How can we sing when the light grows so dim?
**P: You are the light of the world;
be a light in our darkness, O Christ.**
L: Find us in the nighttime of grief,
illumine the pathways through our loss,
and guide us toward the dawn.
**P: You are the light of the world;
be a light in our darkness, O Christ. Amen.**

Hymns
(possibilities)

Come, thou long expected Jesus	HWB 178
Comfort, comfort, O my people	HWB 176
The Lord is my light	STJ 97
Don't be afraid	STJ 105

Silent reflection

Unison prayer
(based on Job 38:19 and John 1:4)

Which is the way to the home of the light, O God?
When will we know the rising of joy?

You have set the patterns of the night and the day,
    you are the life that is light to all people.
Come to us now, O God,
    and to all who know where the darkness lives.
Come, and lead us to the home of the light. Amen.

Hymn
Our darkness is never darkness   STJ 101

Stories of the light
Each passage is read slowly and meditatively, singing "Our darkness" (STJ 101) twice after each silence.

The light of creation—Genesis 1:1-5
(silence, followed by "Our darkness")

The light of the exodus—Exodus 13:17-22
(silence, followed by "Our darkness")

The light of prophecy—Isaiah 25:6-9
(silence, followed by "Our darkness")

The light of hope—Luke 1:46-55
(silence, followed by "Our darkness")

Special music and/or liturgical dance
Consider an ensemble for "Nothing is lost on the breath of God" (STS 121).

A ritual of remembering

On this night we light candles to remember
    those whom we have loved and lost.
We remember their faces and their voices.
We remember their names and offer them now

with our voices raised, or in the silent spaces of our hearts.
(allow names to be spoken aloud)
For these precious lives and the memories we carry
we give you thanks, O God.

On this night we light candles to remember
the loss of relationships, the loss of jobs,
the loss of health.
We come to gather up the pain from our past
and offer it to God, asking that from God's hands
we might receive the gift of peace.
(silent reflection)
Refresh, restore, and reconcile us, O God;
lead us into your future.

On this night we light candles to remember
the light bearers who have stood with us
in the disbelief, the anger, the tears, the silences.
We remember their faces, their voices, their touch.
We remember their names, and offer them now
with our voices raised, or in the silent spaces of our hearts
(allow names to be spoken aloud)
May your eternal love surround and sustain
these Christ-like companions on the way.

O God, as we now bring these candles to flame,
remind us of your light that shines
into all the dark places of our lives and the world. Amen.

People may light and float candles in the bowls as offerings of prayer to the One who sent his Son to be light of the world.

Silent reflection

Sending hymn
(possibilities)

Creator of the stars of night	HWB 177
Sun of my soul	HWB 654
All praise to thee, my God	HWB 658

Sending

    May the blessing of light be upon you,
    Light without and light within.
    May the presence of God enfold and comfort you,
        as you watch and wait
        for the coming of the Dawn. Amen.

309 The Longest Night: O Lord, hear our prayer

Welcome and prayer

Hymn
O Lord, hear my prayer   HWB 348

Scripture for meditation
(four readers, with pause between each reading)
> Psalm 130:1-2, 5-6
> Psalm 28:1-2
> Psalm 139:7, 11-12
> Isaiah 9:2-6

Hymn
Through our fragmentary prayers   HWB 347

Psalm of lament*

(silence)

Hymn
Longing for light   STJ 54

Promises of God's light
(readings are followed by response and hymn)

The light of creation—Genesis 1:1-5

> L: Jesus said, "I am the Light of the World,
> **All:**   ***Anyone who follows me will not walk in darkness,***
>   ***but will have the light of life."***
> *You are all we have (STJ 29)*

*For this, a recommended resource is Ann Weems' *Psalms of Lament*
(John Knox Press. 1995). See the preface and Psalm 19, page 34.

The Light of the exodus—Exodus 13: 17-22

L: Jesus said, "I am the Light of the World.

All: *Anyone who follows me will not walk in darkness,*
but will have the light of life."
Keep me safe, O God (STJ 50)

The Light of the prophets—Isaiah 9:2b-6

L: Jesus said, "I am the Light of the World,

All: *Anyone who follows me will not walk in darkness,*
but will have the light of life."
Holy (STJ 15)

The light of hope—Luke 1:46-55

L: Jesus said, "I am the Light of the World.

All: *Anyone who follows me will not walk in darkness,*
but will have the light of life."

Hymn
My soul is filled with joy   STJ 13

Lighting candles

L: From the light God shines into our darkness this night, we light a candle to remember those whom we have loved and lost, or those whom we carry in our hearts because we fear for their futures. We pause to remember their names, their faces, their voices, and the memory that binds them to us in this season.

All: *May God's eternal love surround them.*

L: We light this second candle as a reminder that God's light redeems the pain of separation and loss; the separation of family or friend, the loss of relationship, of job, of health. We pause to gather up the pain of the past and the fear of the future; we offer it all to God, asking that from God's hands we receive the gift of peace.

All: *Refresh, restore, renew us, O God.*

L: We light this third candle to remember ourselves this Christmas time. We pause and remember these past weeks and months: the despair, the anger, the down times, the struggles and defeats. We also remember the hugs and the handshakes, the prayers of those who have stood with us. We give thanks for support we have known and the tears we have shed.

All: *Let us remember that dawn defeats the darkness.*

L: This fourth candle is lit to remember our faith and the gift of hope that the Christmas story offers. Into a dark world, God came in the form of a tiny, vulnerable babe, so that we can know that even in the darkness, God is present. We are never alone.

All: *Let us remember the one who shows the way, who brings the truth, who bears the light.*

Hymn
Infant holy, infant lowly   HWB 206

Sending
Prayer in unison   STJ 182

Benediction
May the God of hope fill us with all joy and peace in believing, that we may abound in hope through the power of the Holy Spirit. Amen.

310 Christmas Eve candlelighting service

Preparations: Gather hymnals and enough candles for each participant. Appoint four candlelighting readers and four other readers. If possible, arrange chairs in a circle with four aisles radiating outward. The advent wreath, with the Christ candle lit but the four advent candles unlit, is in the center of the circle. The room should be darkened except for candlelight and enough other light for people to read. In order to keep the room darkened and the program undisturbed, the hymn numbers can be posted on the wall. No printed program is needed.

Instrumental prelude

Welcome

Tonight we cerebrate the coming of the Messiah, the Son of God, promised to Israel, thrust upon humble parents, and revealed to an unsuspecting world. Tonight we journey with Joseph and Mary to witness the birth of this most holy child.

Now let us remember the days before the coming of Christ, and imagine the world of trouble and turmoil into which Jesus came, a world not unlike the one we still have. Let us remember the hope given to us in the coming of the light.

Hymn
O Come, O Come, Emmanuel   HWB 172

Candlelighter 1
(lights candle from the center and stands near first quadrant)
> There is a light shining in the darkness,
> a light which shines through the Word,
> and the Word is light
> and the light,
> is the
> light
> of the world.

(lights participants' candles in the quadrant while instrumentalists play)

Reader 1

Under the covers of a warm and quiet night
there is a heart that beats with quiet thunder
that shudders under the load of fear
that comes with glimpsing the face of the unknown.

He shivers in the night air as he looks out the window,
wondering how he will manage.
Where is the light?

So many worries ...
No money
No security
No steady income,
only the sweat of his brow and the work of his hands.

But he is lucky.
He is not out there in the streets begging for the mercy of strangers
shivering in chill night air.
But neither is he warm.

How will they manage—
the two of them,
soon to be three ...
so young,
so scared,
so full of "what will happen if ..."?
Will there be light at the end of this tunnel of uncertainty?

Hymn
Oh, how shall I receive thee?   HWB 182

Candlelighter 2

(lights candle from the center and moves near the second section)

There is a light shining in the darkness,
a light that shines through the Word,
and the Word is light
and the light,
is the
light
of the world.

(lights the candles of a second section of participants, instrumentalists play)

Reader 2

They have family nearby
who try to understand and refrain from judging.
But there are questions ...
unasked,
murmurs behind his back,
hands covering,
mouths whispering.

Reader 1

Then he thinks of her. The wonder in her eyes.
The anticipation of things to come.
Her calmness—certain that God is with her.

Eyes follow her down the street.
He's seen them watch and wonder at her.
She grows daily more beautiful
and more full of the wonder of life.
Can there be light for her that he can't see ?

Hymn

Come thou long expected Jesus   HWB 178

Reader 3

> But there was an angel!
> Imagine, an angel!
>
> She said there was one.
> The angel's name was Gabriel.
> How could she mistake an angel
> for anyone else?
>
> It was no one she knew,
> not dressed up,
> not from far away,
> but rather "other-ly"
> from another place entirely ... from heaven
> where there is no fear of what tomorrow will bring,
> where no one asks whether there will be comfort and safety.

Hymn

The angel Gabriel   HWB 180

Reader 4

> As she rested in the words of the angel,
> in the darkness of her room,
> the light flickered within her.
>
> Soon they would travel. Weariness would well up in them.
> And the man and woman would try to remember the words
> given to them by the angel.
>
> So, the man and the woman packed up their food and their
> belongings and headed toward the town of crowds and
> camels, of pushing and travelers looking for shelter. There
> they would find lodging

(reading from where they are standing)

Candlelighter 1:   and food
Candlelighter 2:   and warmth
Candlelighter 1:   and shelter
Candlelighter 2:   and light.

Candlelighter 3

(lights candle from the center and moves near the third section)

> There is a light shining in the darkness,
> a light which shines through the Word,
> and the Word is light
> and the light,
> is the
> light
> of the world.

(light the candles of a third section, instrumentalists play)

Reader 3

> ✓For the angel had promised her a great joy.
> A child of wonder and wisdom.
> A child of grace.
> A child.
>
> The name of the child would be
> the Awaited One
> the Comforter
> the Prince of Peace
> the Promise of God.

Hymn

Comfort, comfort O my people   HWB 176

Reader 2

> And as the man and the woman stumbled wearily
>   into the dark town

there were no smiles of reassurance
with hot food to warm them
or beds ready
with clean linens smelling of sun and wind.
But after the final step was taken
the time arrived.
Waiting not for beds, or linens,

Candlelighter 1:   or warmth
Candlelighter 2:   or shelter
Candlelighter 3:   or comfort
Candlelighter 4:   or light.

Hymn:
Lo how a Rose e'er blooming   HWB 211

Reader 3
A miracle ...
an every day miracle
that was made miraculous
by the touch of God!

Reader 1
The man stared at the wonder before him.
What strange and holy waves were they,
that cast this child on the shores of their lives?
To be part of such a moment—
surely it was never before like this
for anyone.

Hymn
Infant holy, Infant lowly   HWB 206

Reader 4
An everyday miracle
but more.

The woman nestled the babe to her breast,
as if there were nothing in all the world
but the child—

Candlelighter 1:   no chickens underfoot
Candlelighter 2:   no musty straw to sneeze away
Candlelighter 3:   no drafty darkness
Candlelighter 1:   just warmth
Candlelighter 2:   just shelter
Candlelighter 3:   just comfort
Candlelighter 1:   just light.

Candlelighter 4
(lights candle from the center and moves near the last section)

There is a light shining in the darkness,
a light which shines through the Word,
and the Word is light
and the light,
is the
light
of the world.
(lights the candles of the last section of participants, instrumentalists play)

Reader 1
There they lay,
Whole and complete.
The man wondered at the gentle sounds and soft breathing
when suddenly a joy, so deep it wound around his heart,
wafted out of the cracks in the walls,
soared high into the night,
and cracked the darkness.

Hymn
Break forth, O beauteous heavenly light   HWB 203

Reader 2

> The night was changed—
> no longer a waiting, shapeless presence,
> but a time of holiness and awe.

> Even those in the fields
> were shaken by the shattered darkness.
> A rent in the sky appeared
> and angel song filled the night-shrouded hills.

Hymn

Angels we have heard on high   HWB 197

Reader 4

> The darkness could not hold the light.
> Light poured out over shepherds
> and sheep
> and rolled over the town,
> pushing before it those who had no love for the town,
> its crowds and its noise,
> and pulling in its wake, wanderers from the world's edge.

> All to see the babe—
> the Word become flesh.
> the light of the world—

Candlelighter 1:   bringing hope
Candlelighter 2:   bringing peace
Candlelighter 3:   bringing love
Candlelighter 4:   bringing joy.

Hymn

Joy to the world   HWB 318 (all verses)

Reader 1

And the man leaned against the dark of the stable wall,
his head resting on the rough surface,
hands limp with relief.
The shepherds had gone,
leaving behind gifts, and memories of faces
touched by holy light.
Wisps of excitement still hung in the air
and joy wrapped in garlands around the sleeping pair.

He watched them sleep,
breathing low
and soft
wrapped together in straw and silence—
the light of God shining in and around them.

Candlelighter 1: There is a light shining in the darkness,
Candlelighter 2: a light which shines through the Word,
Candlelighter 3: and the Word is light
Candlelighter 4: and the light is the light of the world.

Hymn
Silent night   HWB 193 (all verses)

311 Ash Wednesday: We pour out our brokenness

This service offers an extended time for confession, focusing on what have been called "the seven deadly sins"—including their passive forms.

Visual environment: a table draped in a neutral-colored cloth (gray, tan, off-white, or a combination); seven clear glass containers of varied shapes, each two-thirds full of a different color of sand, arranged in the center of the worship table; a large, empty clear glass bowl at one end of the table, with small white or off-white votive candles arranged near it; and a tall, empty, clear glass container at the other end.

Gathering

As worshippers arrive, they are met at the door by leaders holding small clay containers filled with ashes. The leaders mark the foreheads of those who choose to participate, smudging ashes in the form of a cross and repeating, "Remember that you are dust, and to dust you will return." Worshippers then enter the sanctuary in silence. After all have arrived, a flute (or other instrument) plays a minor melody such as "Out of the depths I cry to you" (HWB 133) or "From the depths of sin" (HWB 136).

Call to worship *(based on Joel 2:12-13; Psalm 34:17)*

> L: Rend your hearts and not your clothing.
> Return to the Lord, your God,
> **P: for the Lord is gracious and merciful,**
> **slow to anger,**
> **and abounding in steadfast love.**
> L: Even now, says the Lord,
> return to me with all your heart,
> **P: with fasting, with weeping,**
> **and with mourning.**

All: *When the righteous cry for help,*
        the Lord hears
        and rescues them from all their troubles. Amen.

Opening prayer

Merciful God, you call us to turn away from sin and death
and turn toward your gracious love.
Grant us courage to see ourselves with fearless honesty
and to trust in your unfailing forgiveness. Amen.

Hymn

Lord, I am fondly, earnestly longing   HWB 514

Confessing our sins

Scripture reading   Psalm 51:1-9

(read antiphonally by two voices)

Hymn

The sacrifice you accept, O God   HWB 141 (st. 1-4, 7)

Confession ritual: Pouring out our sins

*Two readers read the following prayers antiphonally. A third person
stands behind the table, ready to pour sand with each confession.
Congregation sings stanza 1 of "Oh, Lord have mercy" (STJ 47) after
each pour ritual.*

Prayer of confession

The two readers read HWB 698, followed by silence.

1:   I pour out my sins of pride,
        unbending, unyielding arrogance,
        self-righteous zeal for perfection,
        damning judgments,
        vicious grasp of my own destiny.

2: I pour out my sins of refusal to take my place,
    cowering fear,
    spineless accommodation,
    failure to speak,
    unwillingness to be counted.

Sand is slowly poured from a small container into the large container.
Congregation sings "O Lord, have mercy."

1: I pour out my sins of envy,
    harboring desires for another's ill,
    coveting another's gifts or call,
    betraying confidences,
    giving way to spasms of jealousy.
2: I pour out my sins of lack of desire,
    not yearning for what is good, what is better,
    too self-absorbed to care,
    succumbing to distraction,
    drifting in oblivion.
    (pouring, followed by sung response)

1: I pour out my sins of anger,
    hostile words,
    sullen silence,
    fuming impatience,
    venomous retaliation.
2: I pour out my sins of apathy,
    callous indifference,
    shriveling submission,
    failure to protest injustice
    or to rage against the dying of the light.
    (pouring, followed by sung response)

1: I pour out my sins of lust,
    exploiting another,
    gorging my own satisfaction,

        grasping at passion,
        careless disregard for boundaries.

2:   I pour out my sins of passivity,
        ignoring my body,
        rejecting my senses,
        turning away from touch,
        refusing connection.
   (pouring, followed by sung response)

1:   I pour out my sins of greed,
        devouring the inheritance of others,
        filling my closets,
        giving only what I can spare,
        hoarding smiles or love or mercy.

2:   I pour out my sins of hesitation,
        satisfied with monotony,
        content with shallowness,
        not opening my hands to receive,
        giving without joy.
   (pouring, followed by sung response)

1:   I pour out my sins of gluttony
        demanding more than my share,
        wasting food and people and time,
        grasping achievement,
        consuming beauty or freedom or love.

2:   I pour out my sins of refusing pleasure,
        disregarding my hungers,
        staying utterly sullen,
        never smacking my lips at a feast
        or laughing freely.
   (pouring, followed by sung response)

1:   I pour out my sins of sloth,
        failure of purpose,
        weak tolerance,

          easy distraction,
          sliding into dullness.

2:   I pour out my sins of overwork,
          cramming one more task into the day,
          ignoring my family,
          abusing my body,
          forgetting God.

Ritual of pouring is repeated, followed by "O Lord, have mercy." If some sand overflows the container by this time, it can symbolize the extent of our sin.

1&2: We pour out the sand of our brokenness,
          as we wait upon your grace. *(pause)*

While the next lines of the prayer for mercy are offered, the person who has been pouring sand lifts the large sand-filled container and slowly pours all the sand into the large bowl.

1:   O Lord,
          you do have mercy,
          and so we call upon your grace.
       Pour out cleansing mercy;
          let it wash over me
          and scrub away my iniquity.

2:   Pour out forgiving love;
          let it come down upon my head
          and rinse me clean.

1&2: Pour out renewing grace;

1:      make me holy;

2:      make me whole.

1&2: Through Jesus Christ, we pray. Amen.

Receiving assurance of God's forgiveness

Unison reading by congregation: Psalm 51:10-12

Hymns of assurance
Amazing grace   HWB 143
There's a wideness in God's mercy   HWB 145

Sending

> As those loved and forgiven
>   and promised new life,
> go forth into Lent
>   with courage, hope, and peace.

312 Ash Wednesday: Unless a grain of wheat falls ...

Opening words

> Very truly I tell you, unless a grain of wheat falls into the ground and dies, it remains just a single grain; but if it dies, it bears much fruit. —John 12:24

Hymn

What wondrous love is this   HWB 530 (st. 1-2 unison)

Scripture

(adapted from Psalm 102:1-11)

> **All:** *Hear my prayer, O Merciful One;*
> *let my cry come to you!*
>
> 1: Do not hide your face from me
> in the day of my distress.
>
> 2: Incline your ear to me;
> answer me speedily in the day when I call.
>
> 1: For my days pass away like smoke,
> and my bones burn like a furnace.
>
> 2: My heart is broken,
> the fragments scattered to the winds;
> I am too wasted to eat my bread.
>
> 1: My groanings never cease;
> day and night I call to you.
>
> 2: I am like an owl of the wilderness,
> like a little owl of the waste places.
>
> 1: I lie awake;
> I am like a lonely bird on the housetop.
>
> 2: All day long my fears well up,
> threatening to overwhelm me.
>
> **All:** *Bread turns to ashes in my mouth,*

> *and tears mingle with my drink*
> *because of your indignation and anger.*
> *My days are like an evening shadow;*
> *I wither away like grass.*
> *Hear my prayer, O Merciful One;*
> *let my cry come to you!*

Hymn
O thou, in whose presence   HWB 559

Meditation, followed by silence

Prayer of confession
(from Menno Simons)   HWB 700

Hymn of assurance
My faith looks up to thee   HWB 565 (*hum after st. 1*)

Imposition of ashes
Leaders mark the foreheads of those who choose to participate, smudging ashes in the form of a cross and repeating, "Remember that you are dust, and to dust you will return."

Unison prayer
All Merciful God,
> **you call us forth from the dust of the earth**
> **and name each of us as your beloved children.**
Now look upon us as we enter these Forty Days
> **bearing the mark of ashes:**
> **sign of our mortality,**
> **reminder of our end.**
Bless our journey through the desert of Lent
> **to the waters of rebirth.**
May our fasting be a hunger for justice,
> **our acts of charity, a making of peace,**
> **our prayer, the chant of humble and grateful hearts.**

When we come to Easter and behold the empty cross,
    renew in us the certainty of your unfailing love;
    assure us again that neither life nor death
        can separate us from you.
All that we do and pray is in the name of Jesus,
    our Savior and Lord. Amen.

Hymn
O Love that will not let me go   HWB 577

Worshippers leave in silent contemplation.

313 Maundy Thursday Communion service

*The seven themes and Scripture texts may be printed in an order of
worship. Each worshipper receives a large nail as they enter. The service
begins with seven candles lit, one of which will be extinguished after
each passion story is read. During the service, each reader reads the
Scripture text and the prayer following it, then extinguishes a candle.*

Opening words and prayer

Hymn
Go to dark Gethsemane   HWB 240
(can be played on a recorder instead of sung)

1. Abandonment

Read Matthew 26:36-44

Lord Jesus Christ,
    what an excruciating night—
    sweating drops of blood,
    begging for the cup to pass,
    abandoned by your disciples,
    hoping against hope that your plight might change.

Somehow in the worst of nights
    you were able to perceive the everlasting arms.

What a huge leap to get over that bridge of fear ...
    to get to that place where you could say:
    "Not my will, but yours be done."

In the midst of pending pain,
    you teach us to accompany you ...

✓ to continue to say *yes* to the Lover
✓ and to rest in the eternal arms ...
✓ even in the worst of nights.

Hymn
Beneath the cross of Jesus   HWB 250
(extinguish a candle)

2. Betrayal

Read Matthew 26:14-16, 20-31a, 47-52

You keep offering them bread.
Even when they betray you ...
    even when they desert you ...
    you offer them the cup of forgiveness.
    and invite them to drink.
✓ The holiest of communion is offering grace to those
    who betray and desert.

And when they come to take you away...
    when everything in our hearts cries "Retaliate!"
    you say: "Put up the sword.
    "Lay your weapons down!
    "Violence begets violence ...
✓ ✓ "Love your enemies because God does so."
That is the only reason to love enemies ...
    and that is reason enough.

When will we ever learn?
When will the world learn
    the way of the One who offers bread to his betrayers ...
    the way of the One who forgives those who desert him ...
    the way of the One who says,
    "Put up the sword. Lay your weapons down"?

Hymn of Lament
If the war goes on   STJ 66
(extinguish a candle)

3. Humiliation

Read Matthew 27:27-31

> Bound,
> Slapped,
> Whipped,
> Spit upon,
> Jeered at,
> Rejected,
> Shamed,
> Despised,
> O man of sorrows …
>> you know the worst of human degradation.
> And there you sit with the victims of the world …
>> with the women sold in slave trade,
>> with the children who are abused,
>> with the prisoners who are being tortured.
> There you sit
>> with all who are publicly shamed
>> and privately humiliated.

> And we confess our part in that crowd.
> By the hostility we hold in our hearts,
>> by the words we sling at each other,
>> by the fingers we point,
>> by our attitudes,
>> we, too, enter into the mocking.

And so we pray:

Lord Jesus Christ, have mercy on us.
Kyrie elieson.
Lord Jesus Christ, have mercy on us …
    and grant us peace …
    even as you say:
    "Father, forgive them, for they know not what they do."

Hymn of confession
O Lord, have mercy   STJ 47
(extinguish a candle)

4. Torture

Read John 19:14-19, Mark 15:25-28

Invite people to press their nails against their skin during prayer for suffering humanity. After each intercession, pause for silent or sentence prayers.

Compassionate God, on behalf of an aching world we pray.
We remember ourselves and our loved ones …
We remember the deepest needs of those around us …
We remember those in our church family who are suffering …
We remember those who are homeless and hungry …
We remember victims of war …
We pray for prisoners and captives …
We pray for all who are plagued with depression and grief …
We lift up those whose relationships are frayed
    and whose families are broken …
You are being crucified again and again,
    identifying with all our human suffering and pain.
O Lord Jesus Christ, hear our cries: How long? How long?

Hymn
Were you there   HWB 257
(extinguish a candle)

5. Anguish

Read Matthew 27:45-46, followed by a time of silence
(extinguish a candle)

6. Surrender

Read Luke 23:44-46

Communion at the cross

> Jesus, on the night he was betrayed, offered bread as a
> symbol for his body about to be broken for us, and said,
> "Take eat, this is my body, broken for you." Then he took a
> cup, and after giving thanks, he gave it to them, saying,
> "Drink from this all of you, for this is my blood poured out
> for the forgiveness of sin."

> All ground is level at the cross.
> Here we are all beggars in need of God's gracious love.
> There is no privilege here, only kinship.
> This is the place where we lay down any hostility
>   and all desire for revenge.
> People alienate each other;
>   God brings us back together.
> This holy evening and this holy communion are about
>   the healing forgiveness of Jesus—
>   healing us, healing our relationships,
>   healing, restoring, reconciling the world.
> Let us come to the cross of Jesus
>   and receive the gift of wondrous love.

Participants come to the table to the instrumental music of "What wondrous love is this" (HWB 530).

Prayer of remembrance
> O Lord, Most High,
> on this night of remembered pain and echoing death,
> we pray for fresh resolve to go forth in love.
> We pray for courage and energy and freedom
>> to act in forgiving generosity.
> Because of your act on the cross,
>> we rely on your healing love for all our living
>> and all our relating.
> With deepest humility and praise,
>> we pray in the name of Jesus who trusted fully,
> And who alone is worthy of all our trust. Amen.
> *(extinguish a candle)*

7. Death

Read John 19:28-30; Luke 23:47-49
> *(extinguish final candle)*

Hymn
Christ, we do all adore thee   HWB 105
> *(if possible, sing from memory in the darkness)*

Depart in silence and meditation.

314 Good Friday: What wondrous love

The visual atmosphere for the service is simple and somber. A large standing cross is located in an area where worshippers can easily gather around it. A black cloth is draped across the arms of the cross (possibly with an underlay of crimson cloth so that a tiny border of crimson is visible). On a table nearby, also covered with a black cloth, is a low, flat, sand-filled container. A large white candle is placed at the center of the container and is lit at the beginning of the service. A basket nearby contains enough small white candles for each worshipper.

The congregation may sing all of the suggested music, or a small ensemble (vocal and/or instrumental) may offer some of the selections. During the section "Praying around the cross," the congregation sings continuously while worshippers come forward, light small candles at the Christ candle, and kneel at the cross to offer prayers of intercession. When people are finished praying, they place the lit candle in the sand-filled container, return to their seats, and continue singing with the rest of the congregation.

Gathering

Hymn
What wondrous love is this   HWB 530 (st. 1-2)
 (unison or solo voice)

Opening words
 L: On this day we gather to remember Jesus our Savior
    who loved us and gave himself for us.
   Let us draw near in full assurance
    of God's endless love and mercy.
 P: **To Jesus Christ be thanks and praise—**
    the One carries our sorrows,
    heals our wounds,
    and redeems us from sin and death.

Old Testament reading   Isaiah 53:1-12

Hymn
O sacred Head, now wounded   HWB 252 (st. 1-4)

Opening prayer
> Loving Christ, who died upon a tree,
>> we wait at the cross,
>> remembering a mystery:
> Though our race was undone by a tree,
>> we are now restored by a tree.
> By your death you destroyed death
>> and won us eternal life.
> Strengthen us as we wait with you,
>> opening our hearts to your suffering
>> and the suffering of the world.
> We pray in the name of the Savior of the world. Amen.

Singing at the cross

Alas! And did my Savior bleed?   HWB 253 (st. 1,2)
Ah, holy Jesus   HWB 254
Jesus, remember me   HWB 247
Jesus, keep me near the cross   HWB 617 (st. 1-3)
   (sung slowly in black gospel style)
Open are the gifts of God   HWB 255

Hearing the Word

Gospel reading: Matthew 27:1-60
At the end of verse 50, the Christ candle is snuffed out. Following verse 60, all sit in silence.

Hymn
When I survey   HWB 259

Praying around the cross

Epistle reading: **Hebrews 10:16-23**
   (large white Christ candle is re-lit)

Prayer of confession   **HWB 698**

Hymn
Kyrie eleison   HWB 144
   (silence)

Words of assurance   **HWB 706**

Prayers of intercession around the cross
   (with instrumental music)

Sending

Epistle reading   **Romans 8:31b-39**

Hymns of love to Christ
O Love, that will not let me go   HWB 577
My Jesus, I love thee   HWB 522
Christ, we do all adore thee   HWB 105

Benediction
   May the One who loves us beyond all telling keep us in
   grace until we meet again to celebration the resurrection.
   Go in peace.

Hymn
What wondrous love is this   HWB 530

315 Good Friday service with communion

Service may begin with silence and a prelude.

Welcome and introduction to the day

Hymn
O sacred Head, now wounded   HWB 252

Opening prayer   HWB 743

Scripture readings
Isaiah 53:1-12
   (silence)
John 19:1-7
Hymn: At the cross her vigil keeping   HWB 245 (1-4)
   (sung antiphonally)
John 19:16b-30
Hymn: At the cross her vigil keeping   HWB 245 (5-8)
   (sung antiphonally)

Sermon

Litany
Congregation may kneel if they are able.
   L: Suffering God, hear the prayers of those for whom the
       Lord Jesus was willing to be betrayed. *(pause)* We pray
       for the work of the church. May your people persevere
       in faith and obedience. Grant us grace to accept the
       ministry you have for each of us.
       (silent prayer)
   P: **Lord, have mercy**
   L: Suffering God, we pray for all who are afflicted in body
       and mind. Care for the homeless, for the persecuted, for
       those who know they will soon die. Save those who

face sorrow, those who stand before temptation, and
those who have lost the way.
(silent prayer)

P: **Lord, have mercy**

L: Suffering God, we pray for all who have not received
Christ. Draw to Christ those who have not heard, those
who have lost faith, those who persecute his disciples.
(silent prayer)

P: **Lord, have mercy**

L: Suffering God, we pray for the Jewish people. We
thank you that you chose them to bring the world
salvation. Grant us reconciliation with those whose
Messiah we claim.
(silent prayer)

P: **Lord, have mercy**

L: Suffering God, we pray for all peoples who dwell on
earth. Bless them with food, with justice, with freedom.
Make wars to cease. Bring the reign of your Suffering
Servant to our broken world.
(silent prayer)

P: **Lord, have mercy**

L: We offer you ourselves and our prayers, through the
Holy One, who died for us.

All: *Amen.*

Invitation
Worship planners may choose an appropriate invitation from MM,
pages 74-90.

Hymn

Ah holy Jesus	HWB 254
or Beneath the cross of Jesus	HWB 250

Communion prayer and Lord's Prayer

O God of perfect love, through Jesus, your Son, we have come to know you. In the company of the whole communion of saints, we come before you in this remembrance of Jesus' death with gratitude for your great redemption. You did not spare your only and beloved Son but offered him up to a bitter death. You sent us a friend of sinners and gave us a new covenant. With his stripes we are healed.

O God of bountiful grace, gratitude fills our hearts as we come to the Lord's Table. Let it be a sign to us that you are a God who forgives us gladly and accepts us graciously. Let this bread and cup show forth Christ's work of redemption. In this Holy Supper, make us one with him that we might be steadfast in following our Lord. Send your Spirit to sanctify our hearts so that we might praise our Redeemer and taste his presence now and evermore. Let the bread we break and the cup we drink be a communion of the body and blood of Christ. Hear us for his sake, in whose name we pray, Our Father …

The distribution of the elements may be singly after each of the following prayers or together after both. During the words of institution, the bread and cup may be held aloft.

Words of institution for the bread

For I received from the Lord what I also handed on to you, that the Lord Jesus on the night when he was betrayed took a loaf of bread, and when he had given thanks, he broke it and said, "This is my body that is for you. Do this in remembrance of me."

Prayer of thanks for the bread

Bless, O Christ, the bread that we break.
Make it the bread of our holy communion with you.

Open our eyes that we might see you by faith,
> on the cross, our reconciliation with God.
May your immeasurable act of generosity
> draw us to love you and serve you always. Amen.

(at the beginning of the distribution of the bread)
Eat, beloved, eat the Lord's bread.

Words of institution for the cup

In the same way he took the cup also after supper, saying, "This cup is the new covenant in my blood. Do this as often as you drink it in remembrance of me." For as often as you eat this bread and drink the cup, you proclaim the Lord's death until he comes.

Prayer of thanks for the cup

O Lamb of God, you shed your blood on the cross for us.
Praised be your holy name for your grace and love.
Bless this cup, O Lord.
Make it the communion of your blood,
> so that we may find rest for our souls
> and joy for our journey. Amen.

(at the beginning of the distribution of the cup)
Drink, beloved. Drink the Lord's Cup.

(silence)

Post-Communion prayer
Good Friday prayer   MM p. 98

Hymn
When I survey   HWB 260

Postlude and personal meditation

316 Good Friday service: Stations of the cross

Stations of the cross is a prayer of movement. Arrange art pieces representing the stages of Jesus' passion around the building or outside. Arrange for Scripture readers and leaders, perhaps different ones for each station. Worshippers move from station to station for prayers. The space can also be set up for individual or family worship on Good Friday, with prayers posted at each station and recorded music.

Gathering

Call to worship: John 3:10, 16, 17

Opening Prayer

L: Lord Jesus Christ, Savior of the world,
     ✓ as we journey with you to the cross,
        help us remember this as a journey of love.
    May we accept the love you offer
        and, in that love, follow you more closely.

P: Open our hearts to hear your Word,
       to receive your love,
       and to enter the mystery
   ✓   **of your passion, death and resurrection.**

Station 1: Jesus prays in the garden

Scripture: Luke 22:41-46

L: Jesus, we see you in the dark of night, praying.
    You are struggling to do your Father's will.
    Even as you agonize in your sorrow,
       your disciples are weary and fall asleep.
    Yet God sends an angel to give you strength.

P: Jesus, wake us from our sleep.
Give us courage to face our fears.
Strengthen us when we are weak.
Teach us to prayerfully trust in you. Amen.

Station 2: Jesus is betrayed and arrested

Scripture: Mark 14:43-46

L: Jesus, you are facing an angry crowd.
One of your disciples turns against you
and rejects your love.
His kiss betrays you to your enemies.

P: Jesus, we come proclaiming our love for you
in our prayers and worship.
But often our words and outward show of affection
conceal hearts that easily turn from you.
Forgive us.
Help us to love you with our heart, mind,
body and soul. Amen.

Station 3: Jesus is condemned by the Sanhedrin

Scripture: Matthew 26:62-66

L: Jesus, your words are blasphemy to the high priest.
He does not know who you are.
He cannot see that God is present in you
and in the works you do.
And so you are accused of great wickedness.

P: Jesus, our vision is limited too.
It is hard, almost impossible,
to see who you truly are.
Open our eyes;
set us free from our blindness,

reveal yourself to us in all your grace and power,
so we may follow you in truth. Amen.

Station 4: Peter denies knowing Jesus

Scripture: Matthew 26:69-75

L: Jesus, you told Peter
that he would deny you three times.
He swore it would never happen;
He was so sure of his love that he even said
he would be willing to die for you.
Yet you knew Peter better than he knew himself.
When morning came and the cock crowed,
Peter saw the bitter truth.

P: **Jesus, we have promised to follow you,
to serve you all the days of our life.
But we have also denied you.
We are sometimes afraid to speak the truth
or acknowledge you when we are with others.
But you keep on loving us.
We love you, too. Amen.**

Station 5: Jesus is condemned by Pilate

Scripture: Luke: 23:13-15, 23-24

L: Jesus, when the crowd shouts "guilt,"
Pilate perceives "innocence."
But the crowd insists,
and Pilate fears his own conscience.
Too weak to resist them,
Pilate gives in and hands you over to be crucified.

P: **Jesus, we have been threatened by crowds;
sometimes we fear what those around us will say
or do.**

Fill us with courage to speak the truth.
Give us compassion for outcasts.
And keep us close to you. Amen.

Station 6: Jesus is scourged and crowned with thorns

Scripture: Mark 15:16-19

L: Jesus, the soldiers mock you.
In their eyes, you are weak and powerless.
They cannot understand you
because, without God, your reign cannot be seen.
You are treated as an imposter,
caught in a lie.

P: **Jesus, our eyes are dim.**
Like the soldiers,
we cannot truly see you without the eyes of faith.
Help us understand your upside-down kingdom—
where our weakness is your strength,
and our powerlessness is God's glory.
Come and reign among us, now and always. Amen.

Station 7: Jesus takes up his cross

Scripture: John 19:16b-17

L: Jesus, you set out holding the wood of the cross
as Isaac carried wood up the mountain with his father.
But unlike Isaac,
you carry all the burdens of the world
and you are the sacrifice.

P: **Jesus, your sentence is unjust;**
you carry the cross,
and you carry our burdens.

There is no greater love than this:
>to lay down one's life for one's friend.
We offer thanks and praise,
>for you are worthy of our love and honor. Amen.

Station 8: Simon of Cyrene helps Jesus

Scripture: Luke 23 :26

L: Jesus, you are weary and weak from torture.
In the Garden of Gethsemane
>God sent an angel to strengthen you.
Now Simon, a human servant,
>comes to relieve your burden.

P: **Jesus, give us strength for the journeys we must take.**
Open our eyes to see the needs
>**of those who walk with us.**
Give us generous hearts to ease another's pain.
Walk beside us and show us your way. Amen.

Station 9: Jesus meets the weeping women.

Scripture: Luke 23:27-31

L: Jesus, when you spoke to the women,
>you asked them not to weep for you
>but for all who are vulnerable and weak.
Even in your suffering,
>you turn away from your own grief to reach out to
>>others.

P: **Jesus, our world is full of terror:**
>**children suffer,**
>**the innocent are accused;**
>**and the righteous lose hope.**
With you we weep
>**and long for justice and peace.**

Hear our cry for mercy
for ourselves and your world. Amen.

Station 10: Jesus is crucified

Scripture: Luke 23:33-38

L: Jesus, even as you suffer,
and the nails pierce your hands and feet,
your words to those who mock and torment you
are words of compassion and forgiveness.
Your heart holds love and mercy for all.
P: **Jesus, your suffering moves us deeply;**
we marvel at your compassion and grace.
When we follow the way of vengeance,
our path goes nowhere.
Forgive our waywardness.
By your wounds, heal us. Amen.

Station 11: Jesus promises paradise to the crucified thief

Scripture: Luke 23:39-43

L: Jesus, you are hanging on the cross between two thieves—
one who makes fun of you and your power,
another who wants to be with you in paradise.
One sees weakness;
the other sees your hidden power
and trusts your promise of everlasting life.
P: **Jesus, look upon us now in our need.**
When our pain is unbearable,
surround us with mercy.
When everything seems hopeless.
keep our faith alive.

Open our eyes to see your kingdom.
Jesus, remember us. Amen.

Station 12: Jesus cares for his mother

Scripture: John 19:25-27

L: Jesus, even in your suffering
    you think of others and entrust them to each
      other's care.
Grant us your promised Spirit to help care for one another.
P: **Jesus, we are now your disciples.**
Join us together as sisters and brothers
    who care for one another and for the world you love.
May the Spirit work in us to enlarge our compassion
    and share your life. Amen.

Station 13: Jesus dies

Scripture: Luke 23:44-47

L: Jesus, you have finished your work,
    and are returning to the One who sent you.
Despite the death clouds that surround you,
    your trust in God remains firm.
P: **Jesus, we also have a purpose in this life.**
Help us to trust in God's love for us
    and commit ourselves into God's care.
May we live for you and others
    so your dying will not be in vain. Amen.

Station 14: Jesus is buried

Scripture: Luke 23:53-56

> L: Jesus, this is your time to rest as you surrender to God.
> We wait with you for the time
> when all things will be made new.
> **P: Jesus, in this time of waiting may we not forget**
> **that God's promises are true.**
> **Life will come out of death.**
> **Grant us patience and strengthen our trust**
> **as we wait for the revelation**
> **of your power and glory. Amen.**

Closing

Scripture: Isaiah 52:13–53:12 or Hebrews 10:16-25

Benediction
> Go forth as God's loved and forgiven people
> and wait in hope for the revelation
> of God's power and glory. Amen.

(317) Labor Day: Celebration of Vocations

Invite a few members to prepare testimonies of how they see and serve God in their workplaces. For the worship display, invite all worshippers to bring an object they use at work.

Call to Worship

1: We are the fruit of God's work.

2: Each one of us a marvelous and precious Potter's delight.

1: We are God's handiwork,
　　　reborn in Christ Jesus to be a blessing.

2: Every one of us, woven together in love,
　　　shaped with infinite possibilities,
　　　painted with incredible beauty.

1: We are the work of God's creation.

All: *All of us—touched by grace, saved by faith,*
　　　and beckoned to praise.

Hymn

Many and great, O God	HWB 35
You are the God within life	HWB 537

Reading

Bless the work of our hands, O God	STS 157

Testimonies of God at work

Sung response: Take, O take me as I am	STJ 81

Offering and Offertory

Prayer

Enterprising God, we know that our capacity to work is one of the ways we have been made in your image. You work. And your work is magnificent and worthy of praise!

We pray today for your work in many lives and situations.
(pray for specifics)
We pray for those who are unemployed or laid off.
(pray for specifics)

You call us to make our work part of the worship of our
lives—to press your holy reign into all our daily tasks,
responsibilities and relationships—even our fun.

As we stand now, we continue our prayer for our labors of
all kinds.

Congregation prays HWB 804 in unison.

Scripture readings
Matthew 6:9-13; Genesis 1:31–2:3; Genesis 3:17-19

Sermon

Hymn
Take My Life (vv. 1, 2, 6)   HWB 389

Blessing of our work

Celebration of Vocation Blessing

If possible, gather around the display of objects from your congregation's occupations.

Our work—our vocational calling—is a very significant
aspect of our lives. It is one of the ways God uses us the
most. Let us recognize the many opportunities we have to
join God's work in the world through our work—wherever
it takes us: a job, school, our neighborhood, or our home.

These "tools of our trades" are humble in some ways, yet gallant in others. They symbolize the time, energy, and resources we commit to serving God in our work. This display reminds us that God has given us many talents, many skills, and many opportunities. We seek to use them all wisely.

Join me for a blessing for our work. Let us open our hands in front of us, as a sign of our readiness to receive God's blessing on us and on our work. *(Worshippers open their hands.)*

At our best, O God, the work and the worship of our lives are one—given to you with the whole of ourselves and the whole of our lives.

For children and seniors and everyone in between, men and women, girls and boys, in their jobs with pay and their jobs as volunteers, at work in their homes and at work in your world—we ask your heavenly blessing now, on all that we are, and all that we do. Amen.

Hymn
Take, O take me as I am   STJ 81

Benediction
God is working in and through you.
May your work
    everywhere,
    every day
—be one clear way you see and serve God.
Go in peace.

318 All Saints' Day service: The circle unbroken

If possible, arrange participant chairs in a circle around the table. On the table arrange leaves, Christ candle from Easter, rocks, glass bowl of water, glass blocks, and unlit tea lights.

As worshippers arrive, invite each to take a tea light and join the circle near the table. They may also take off their shoes as they enter this holy ground of saints and angels, of the living and the dead.

You may wish to begin the service by ringing a bell or a singing bowl

Gathering
L: The Lord be with you.
P: And also with you.
L: As we meet together on this holy day,
  let us join together in prayer:

All: *Gracious God,*
  in this season of fullness and completion,
  on this evening when deep gratitude and deep
    sorrow mingle,
  we praise you for all living and all dying.
We thank you for that great circle
  in which we are united with all those
  who have gone before us.
Bring us, Eternal One, to the day
  when you will free our eyes from tears,
  our feet from stumbling,
  when we shall walk before you
  in the land of the living. Amen.

Hymn
Now on land and sea descending   HWB 655

Remembering who God is and who we are

Psalm 90	HWB 819
Hymn: O God, our help in ages past	HWB 328

Poem: "Herbst" (Autumn) by Rainer Maria Rilke[1]
Poem: "Leaves" by Gunilla Norris[2]

Remembering our loved ones

Participants light tea lights, speaking the names of people they wish to remember. Leader may ring the bell or the singing bowl after each.

Affirming faith

Scripture reading: Hebrews 11:1-3, 8-16, 32-39; 12:1-2

Prayers of intercession

Introduce a time of silence to recall the events of this day and pray for the church and for the world.

Sending

Hymn: Great God, we sing	HWB 639

Benediction

> May the God who blessed us with loved ones,
> encircle our grief and memory and
> enrich us while we have life:
> eager as we are to meet again in glory.

1. This poem, easily found on the web, could be read first in German and then in English.
2. From *Journeying in Place: Reflections from a Country Garden*, Belltower, New York, © 1994 pp. 3-5.

319 All Saints' Day: Memory

Invite people to prepare short two- or three-sentence memories appropriate to the prayers below.

This service can stand alone or fit into a regular Sunday worship service.

L: Memory is the primary handle that connects us to the roots of our faith. Memory keeps the significance of past events relevant and meaningful for the present. On this day of remembering, some political leaders want us to consider the sacrifice of our soldiers who have died and are dying in battle. While we value them and the freedom we have, we also mourn the violence of our world and pray for alternative pathways to peace.

     What do we remember today in this congregation?

All: **We remember the faith of our ancestors.**
(sharing about a peacemaking ancestor)

All: **We remember the conscientious objectors.**
(sharing from a C.O., or one who knows one)

All: **We remember the refugees.**
(sharing about a refugee experience)

All: **We remember the activists.**
(sharing from one who has taken peaceful public action)

All: **We remember the prisoners.**
(sharing from former inmate or prison volunteer)

L: We remember Jesus:
All: *who was born into a world of violence and hatred,*
but brought a message of peace and hope.

L: We remember Jesus:
All: *whose way of love so infuriated the powers*
that they murdered him with a violent death upon
a cross.

L: We remember Jesus:
All: *who could have resisted violently,*
yet chose to give his life peacefully.

L: We remember Jesus
All: *who calls us to follow in his footsteps of peace.*

L: We remember the risen Christ
All: *who disarms the powers of death*
and proclaims the power of everlasting love.
Thanks be to God. Alleluia. Amen.

320 Intercessory prayer: Let your light shine

As a visual, consider using a large Christ candle and smaller floating candles, arranged in the worship center.

> L: Jesus Christ, Light of the world,
> > we sing your praise,
> > and we revel in your love.
> > Let your light shine among us.
> > > *(Christ candle is lit)*
>
> All: **We give thanks for all the light**
> > **that shines in our lives:**
> 1: our families who love us,
> 2: friends who care for us,
> 3: the body of Christ that binds us together,
> 1: the beauty of the created world,
> 2: meaningful work,
> 3: and time for rest and Sabbath.
> All: **We thank you that at every day's dawning**
> > **we receive the fresh gift of your love and light,**
> > **and at each day's closing**
> > **we rest in the comfort of your light and peace.**
> L: We pray for the light that has illumined our lives
> > to be shed abroad in all the world—

(As each intercession is offered, light a small floating candle and place it in the large bowl of water.)

> —in distant countries and faraway places where bombs
> > explode and life seems cheap;
> —in our nation where racism destroys the dignity of many,
> > and reconciliation is achingly slow in coming;
> —in our towns and neighborhoods where families are
> > hungry or abused, and hope is scarce;

—among those who mourn and grieve,
  for whom the light seems dim;
—among those in pain, physically, mentally, spiritually,
  for whom daily life is a struggle;
—among those called our enemies, whether by our nation's
  choice or our own;
—and on Planet Earth, where harmful choices and
  practices threaten to destroy our home.

All: *Jesus Christ, Light of the world,*
  shine on us and your world today,
  and make us bearers of your light and love. Amen.

321 Evening song and prayer service: Hide me in the shadow of your wings

Visual environment: On a central table, arrange clusters of candles of varying heights and light them before the service begins. Place a large white pillar candle (Christ candle) on a stand or tall candleholder in front of the table and leave it unlit until the hymn of light is sung. Set baskets of small individual candles near the unlit candle.

During the prayers of intercession, worshippers may light small candles at the Christ candle and place them into sand-filled containers set nearby—symbolizing the offering of our prayers into God's care. They may stand or kneel near a large standing cross (or around a cross lying on the floor), offering silent prayers of intercession.

The service should be led in a gentle, leisurely manner that creates a spacious place for silence, reflection, and prayer.

Gathering

Prelude

Opening hymns
All praise to thee   HWB 658
    (st. 1 in unison; st. 2-3 in canon; st. 4 in harmony)
Thank you for the night   STS 86

Scripture reading: Psalm 61:1-4; 57:1-3; 17:6-8; 57:9-11
    (with sung "Alleluia" [HWB 101] after each section)

Prayer
    God who holds us in loving care each day and night,
        we give thanks for the blessings of this day:
        the beauty of the earth,

the care of family and friends,
the challenges of work,
and unexpected glimpses of your nearness.
We give thanks for your presence in difficult moments:
tension in relationships,
anxieties about our jobs,
worries about family and friends,
uncertainty about the future,
disappointment in our failures.
As we come before you in worship,
hold us close to your heart;
set us free from fear,
and grant us your peace.
We pray in the name of Jesus. Amen.
(silence)

Hearing The Word

Hymn: O joyous light of glory   STJ 116
(large candle is lit during the hymn)
Scripture reading: Exodus 19:3-8a
Hymn: The care the eagle gives her young   HWB 590
Scripture reading: Psalm 91
Hymn: Thy holy wings   STJ 118
Scripture reading: Luke 13:31-35
(silence)
Hymn: Under his wings   MH 575
Hymn: There is a place of quiet rest   HWB 5

Responding in prayers of intercession
(sung response: "Kyrie eleison " [HWB 152])

In the shadow of your wings, loving God,
we bring to you our concerns for our world,
our communities, our churches and ourselves.
(specific concerns, followed by sung response)

We pray for those who keep peace in difficult places,
    for leaders of nations,
    for tribes and peoples at war,
    for local leaders seeking justice for the poor.
    (specific concerns, followed by sung response)

We pray for those who lead the church,
    for denominational and conference leaders,
    for pastors, teachers, and youth sponsors,
    for aid workers and missionaries
    and all who serve the church
        in lonely or dangerous places.
    (specific concerns followed by sung response)

We pray for ourselves and those near to us,
    our families, friends and neighbors,
    those whom we struggle to love and understand,
    and all who are ill or grieving or in despair.
    (specific concerns, followed by sung response)

Keep us all, dear Lord, in your watchful care;
    guard us as the apple of your eye,
    and shelter us in the shadow of your wings.
We pray in the name of our Savior, Jesus Christ. Amen.

Hymn: Our Father   HWB 554

Prayers are offered around the cross for all to find refuge in the shadow of God's wings. After each prayer, "Come and fill our hearts with your peace" (STJ 59) may be used as a response.

Sending
Hymn: The peace of the earth be with you   STJ 77

Index for Worship Use

A

All Saints' Day / Eternity
    Sunday, 236-39, 318-19
Advent, 169-78, 308-9
Affirmation of Faith, 16, 126-40,
    177, 189, 199, 217-18, 227-28
Ascension Day, 221-23
Ash Wednesday, 192-94, 311-12

B

Back-to-school, 262
Benedictions, 154-78, 190-91,
    203, 219-20, 222-23, 232
Blessings (of people and
    animals), 251-74, 290-93,
    302-3

C

Calls to worship, 1-33, 169, 170,
    182, 184, 188, 192, 195, 212-
    16, 221, 224-26, 228, 231,
    275, 278, 281
Christmas Eve, 179-81, 310
Christmas, 182-83, 308-9
Confession, 50-75, 115, 174, 185,
    193, 198, 200-2
Commissioning (of people),
    297-307

**Credentialing ministers, 31,
    297-300**

D

Dedications (of things), 288-96

E

Easter, 212-20
Epiphany, 184-87
Eternity Sunday / All Saints'
    Day, 236-39, 318-19
Evening Prayers, 61, 248-50, 321

F

Funerals, 236

G

Gathering, 1-33, 169-70, 182,
    184, 188, 192, 195, 212-16,
    221, 224-26, 228, 231, 275,
    278, 281
Good Friday, 206, 209-11, 314-16
Graduation, 263-65
Ground-breaking, 294-95

H

Holy Week, 204-11

L
Labor Day, 317
Laments, 275-87
Lent, 195-203
Lord's Supper, 115-21, 207-8, 315
Longest Night, 308-9

M
Maundy Thursday, 206-8, 313
Morning Prayers, 61, 240-47
Mothers' Day, 33

O
Offering, 135, 141-53, 187, 234-35
Opening prayers, 2, 4, 6, 10, 19, 22-30, 32-33, 169-70, 182, 184, 188, 192, 195, 212-16, 221, 224-26, 228, 231, 275, 278, 281

P
Palm Sunday, 204-5
Parent/child dedication, 256-59
Peace Sunday, 12, 58, 59, 100, 109
Pentecost, 224-32
Praise, 4-6, 9, 20, 34-49
Prayers
    of invocation, 19, 23-28, 32-33, 171-72, 186, 226, 233, 276
    of healing, 76-80, 183, 196-97

of illumination (pre-sermon and/or scripture), 81-91, 180, 230
of intercession, 92-100, 183, 260, 280, 283-84
of petition, 101-10, 173, 175-76, 180, 183, 194, 229, 277, 279, 282
Trinity, 10, 111-14
for communion, 115-21
for congregational sharing, 122
of thanksgiving (see praise), 4, 5, 6, 9, 21, 34-49
public or government houses, 123-24
for heritage Sunday, 125
mealtime, 253-54
Prayer service, 320

R
Responding, 126-40, 177, 189, 199, 217-18, 227-28

S
Sending, 154-68, 178, 190-91, 203, 219-20, 222-23, 232

T
Tranfiguration, 188-91
Trinity Sunday, 233-35

W
Wedding, 268-70

Topical Index

A

Abundance, 64, 117, 143, 147, 151

Acceptance, 1, 15, 201

Achievement, 102

Adoration, 196

Agriculture, 4, 5, 36, 46, 157, 160

AIDS/HIV, 96, 280

Angels, 38, 40

Anger, 98, 279

Anxiety, 82, 101, 145, 198, 277

Art, 36, 49

Assurance, 1, 33-34, 64, 72, 117, 134, 203

B

Baptism, 83, 121, 151, 185, 225

Beatitudes, 50, 194

Birth, 134, 172, 175-76, 179, 181, 218, 256, 279

Blessing, 5, 41, 251-74

Blindness, 118

Body (human) 9, 24, 27, 30, 32-33, 54, 61, 76-79, 81, 83, 87, 117, 139, 161, 250

Body of Christ, 26, 54, 135

Bread, 116-17, 119

Breath, 114

Broken, 200

Buildings, 27, 294-96

Business Meetings, 26, 27

Busyness, 28, 51, 77-78, 82, 169-70

C

Calling, 29, 104, 170, 173, 252

Celebration, 138

Children

(about) 16, 45, 79, 82, 102, 110, 121, 175-76, 180, 194, 256-61, 280, 283, 304-5

(for) 121, 128, 206, 262, 286, 288, 292

Church, 16-17, 19, 95, 99, 103, 112, 117, 138, 199, 212, 285, 294-96, 306

Comfort, 12, 19, 34, 98, 247, 276

Communion, 115-21, 207-8, 315

Community, 21, 100, 156, 158

Confession, 50-75, 115, 250

Conflict, 69, 159, 156

Contrast community, 286

Control, 103

Courage, 32, 57, 155, 202

Covenant, 6, 119, 121, 200

Creation (God), 2, 4, 10, 22, 25,

29, 32, 36-39, 46, 48, 62, 83,
92, 98, 111, 114, 139, 160,
224, 227, 244
Creation (human), 61
Credentialing, 298, 299
Cross, 54, 77, 89, 126, 160, 214,
281

D
Dance, 9, 40, 190-91
Darkness, 186, 218, 255, 281,
308-9
Death, 212, 236, 276, 297
Decision making, 26-27, 84, 92,
100, 285
Desire, 6, 117, 173
Despair, 19, 92, 101, 176, 211,
218, 255
Direction, 19, 27
Disaster, 98
Discipleship, 3, 66, 68, 74, 84,
104, 108, 115, 136, 138, 140,
175, 244, 286
Disease, 78
Divorce, 287
Doubt, 19, 57, 200
Dreams, 64-65, 83, 85, 90, 279

E
Ears, 81, 161, 242
Easter, 89, 212-20
Education, 304-5
Emotions, 76, 79, 85
Empire, 68, 103
Enemies, 12, 34, 62, 68, 75, 95,
103, 105-6, 109, 277

Enough, 48, 110
Environment, 86, 93
Eternal life, 5, 196
Eternity, 31, 171, 236-39
Evil, 67, 177
Evening, 61, 248-50, 321
Eyes, 31, 48, 81, 161

F
Faith, 163, 171, 177, 201, 219
Faithfulness, 29
Families, 62, 80, 146, 290-91
Fear, 34, 51, 55, 66, 73, 98, 110,
158, 174, 198, 200, 249, 277,
279, 284
Feast, 116, 121, 147
Food, 253-54
Forgiveness, 63, 158, 210, 241
Freedom, 88, 158, 188
Friendship, 35, 158
Future, 18, 55, 65, 83, 101, 200

G
Generosity, 110, 153, 150
Gifts, 49, 102, 110, 114, 116, 135,
140-153, 187
God
    acts of, 5, 20
    alpha and omega, 29
    authority of, 129, 132, 225
    blessing of, 200, 224
    breath of, 11
    deliverance, 65, 84
    empathy of, 278
    eternal, 26, 31
    face of, 21, 177, 202

faithfulness of, 1, 5, 103, 138
feminine, 24, 33, 79
forgiveness of, 197
glory of, 25, 187-88
goodness of, 4, 23
grace of, 2, 6, 26, 61, 160, 210
greatness of, 7, 38, 41, 65, 103, 148, 224, 252
guidance from, 19, 117
holiness of, 7
love of, 2, 20, 59, 67, 71, 77, 90, 156, 165, 210, 237, 248, 276
mercy of, 23, 58, 62, 65, 69-70, 109, 111
mystery of, 2, 4, 31, 48
names for 7, 10, 12-13, 22, 33, 49, 62, 68, 70, 92-93, 104, 129, 179-80, 190, 195-96, 236, 253, 256, 270
presence of, 2, 5, 21-23, 28, 31, 67, 77-78, 87, 103, 128, 174, 183, 186, 188, 225, 228, 281
promises of, 65, 200
protection, 104
providence, 12, 21, 73, 88, 103, 132, 135, 138, 148, 151, 162, 234, 250
power, 46, 212, 224-25, 231
salvation, 177, 200
voice of, 7, 30, 32
will of, 22, 103
wisdom of, 6, 32

Good Friday, 89, 206, 209-11
Gossip, 76
Government, 73, 89, 91, 93, 123-24, 132
Gospel/good news, 32, 68, 175, 214
Global church, 212
Glory, 102, 182, 184
Grace, 52, 209
Grief, 92, 96, 98-99, 130, 183, 215, 275-76, 279, 282, 284, 308-9
Guidance, 26-27, 29

H
Hands, 161
Healing, 40, 44, 65, 76-80, 92, 100, 139, 154, 156
Heart, 80-81
Hell, 211
Holy Spirit, 5, 34, 67, 70, 73, 95, 100, 107, 111, 114, 150, 158, 188-89, 199, 222, 224-32, 244, 275
Heritage, 3, 99, 125, 138, 318-19
Hope, 1, 8, 13, 55-56, 70, 83, 98, 105, 137-38, 163-64, 175, 184, 198, 213, 216, 219-20
Honor, 84
House, 27
Human condition, 27-29, 50-52, 71, 74, 80, 130, 174, 245
Hunger (physical), 66, 147, 280
Hunger (spiritual), 120, 130
Humility, 66, 74, 103, 137, 152, 194, 251

Hypocrisy, 193

I
Idols, 102, 192-93
Illness, 78
Imagination, 48-49, 89, 163,
Injustice, 58, 61-62, 101
Inner life, 5, 104, 107, 170
Intellect, 84, 87, 102
Interfaith, 123-24, 265
Intergenerational, 45, 102, 264,
    304
Intuition, 84

J
Jesus Christ
    anointed, 154
    ascension of, 221-23
    baptism of, 185
    birth of, 172, 175-76, 179,
        181, 184
    death and resurrection, 119,
        133, 138, 143, 146, 204,
        209, 211-20, 313-14, 316
    forgiveness, 54, 136
    foundation, 27
    host, 11
    high priest, 61
    human nature of, 61
    incarnation, 60, 174, 181
    lamb of God, 40
    life of, 108, 113
    love of, 181, 237
    names for, 80, 113, 115, 119-
        20, 127, 142, 159, 177,
        180, 184, 199, 205, 211,
        221
    nature of, 194, 196
    peace of, 73, 159
    power, 102
    reconciling love, 53, 106,
        160, 162
    redeemer, 74, 114, 234
    Spirit of, 75
    suffering of, 78, 82, 192,
        204-10
    teachings, 103, 126
    transfiguration of, 189-90
    the center, 104
Joy, 2, 4, 9-10, 25, 86, 142-43, 169,
    184, 215, 219-20
Journey, 121, 123, 140, 155, 186,
    192
Justice, 32, 39, 62, 70, 105, 109,
    123-24, 155, 158, 207, 251

K
Kingdom, 4-5, 130
Knowledge, 31, 102

L
Leaders, 297-307
Leadership, 89, 93-94, 103, 186,
    251-52
Light, 3, 27, 92, 101, 159, 184,
    187-88, 320
Loneliness, 156, 159, 211, 279
Lord's Prayer, 83, 95, 118
Lord's Supper, 115-21, 207-8,
    315

Love, 20, 22, 31, 53, 234-35

M

Magi, 184, 187
Marriage, 96, 268-72, 286
Mary, 175, 178-79
Materialism, 51, 57, 68, 89, 144
Maturity, 29
Mealtime, 253-54
Mercy, 42, 251
Ministry of all, 95, 135, 251-52,
    297, 306-7
Missional, 26, 85, 178, 201
Morning, 11, 40, 61, 240-47
Money, 62, 102, 132, 141, 144,
    145, 147, 247
Mother's Day, 33
Mystery, 14, 118, 169-70
Music, 35-36, 43, 47, 90, 232

N

Natural disasters, 284
Nature, 4, 36, 38
Neighbors, 58, 62, 80, 93, 96, 277
New creation, 55

O

Obedience, 26
Openness, 6, 21
Oppression, 42, 59, 61, 66, 95,
    101, 139
Other gods, 177, 193

P

Parents, 256-59, 261, 264
Patriotic holiday, 129-30
Peace/Shalom, 12, 18, 22, 32,
    36, 45, 61, 67, 77, 92, 94-95,
    105, 151, 155-56, 158, 198
Peace Sunday, 12, 58-59, 105,
    109
Peacemakers, 58, 61, 69-70, 105,
    108, 130
Perfectionism, 51
Pets, 273-74
Play, 21
Praise, 28, 34-49, 221, 228, 232
Poverty, 94-95, 101, 103, 133
Power, 72, 86, 93, 132, 139, 145
Prejudice, 105
Pride, 51, 84
Prophesy, 230

Q

Quiet, 30, 33

R

Refugees, 88
Reconciliation, 70, 109
Reign of God, 4-5, 130
Relationship, 76, 80
Renewal, 29, 170, 176, 183, 190,
    198-99
Resurrection, 152, 252
Righteousness, 69
Risk, 14, 67
Roots, 220

S

Sabbatical, 301-2
Sacred space, 21, 31
Saints, 44, 125, 236-39
Salvation, 41, 68, 74, 84

Scripture, 30, 149, 288-89
Security, 51, 67, 90
Seeking, 21
Service, 82, 92, 137, 194, 222
Shalom (wholeness and peace), 13, 200, 282
Shadows, 186, 192, 206
Silence, 208-9
Sin, 75, 93, 177, 197, 280
Solstice, 255
Sorrow, 25
Speech, 27, 32, 74, 83
Spirit, 10, 81, 85, 150
Spiritual discipline, 107-8,
Spring, 36, 213, 220
Stewardship, 141-53, 232
Strength, 15
Stress, 277
Success, 51, 102
Suffering, 2, 12, 95
Surprise, 179, 182, 191, 226

T
Table, 116, 118, 120-21, 147
Teaching, 42, 67, 102, 305
Temptation, 71
Terrorism, 75, 97
Thanksgiving, 20, 25, 35, 45, 95, 113, 138, 151, 235, 244, 320
Thirst, 58, 120, 147
Thorns, 87
Transformation, 14, 85, 90, 95, 102-3, 107, 188, 190

Transition, 19
Trinity, 10, 114, 140, 165, 185, 191, 233-35, 253
Truth, 62, 159
Trust, 19-20, 29, 110, 113, 131, 134, 245-46, 250

U
Uncertainty, 19, 101, 163, 170, 200
Unity, 16-17, 26, 133

V
Violence, 58-59, 70, 75, 105, 158
Vine, 117, 119
Vision, 31, 72, 190
Voice, 139, 158

W
Waiting, 56, 171-72, 179
War, 50, 59, 212, 238
Water, 30, 65
Weakness, 15, 170
Weariness, 11, 23, 176
Wholeness, 13, 94
Wisdom, 32, 90, 160
Witness, 94, 100, 133, 137-38, 157, 162, 164, 166-67, 171, 178, 189, 207, 216-17, 225
Wilderness, 63, 65
Womb, 134, 172, 185, 244
Women in the Bible, 139
Wonder, 48, 149, 170

Word, 32
Work, 21, 82, 87, 95, 102, 107,
    144, 293, 317
Y
Youth,
    (for) 45, 107, 263-66
    (about), 180, 304
Young Adults, 267

Scripture Index

OLD TESTAMENT

Deuteronomy
6 304

Exodus
15 65

1 Samuel
16:1-13 89

1 Kings
8:22-53 64

2 Kings
2:1-12 189

Job
38:19 308

Psalms
1 86
2 88
9:1-2 20
16:8 132
23 . . . . . 12, 34, 68
29 7
30 . . . . . . 40, 44, 65
31:12 200
33 47
34:17 311
47:6 221
50:1-6 189
61 298
66:1-9 43
72 184
78 304
85:8-13 41
91:1-6 160
93 221
95 9
102:1-11 312
104 . . . . . . 46, 224
119. 142
121 73
122 45
126 91
130 282
131 33
133 . . . . . . 17, 141
137. 278-80
143 65
143:8 246
146 39
148 38
150 57

Isaiah
1:17 59
2:1-4 18
43:1 2
43:1-4 277
43:19 8
49 33
58:9-11 66
60:1-6 184

Joel
2:12-13 311

Amos
5:6 60

Micah
6:8 251

NEW TESTAMENT
Matthew
3:13-17 154
5:3-11 . . . . . 50, 133
5:43-48 . . . . 53, 286
7:1-5 106
14:13-21 77

Mark

4:26-29 4
9:2-9 189

Luke

6:27-31 106
18:8 61

John

1:1-15 84
1:4 308
3 196
3:1-17 134
3:14 82
4:5-42 199
12:24 312
15:1-15 84
17:23 137
20:19-29 57
21:7 40

Acts

2:1-21 230
10:34-43 154

Romans

3:28 165
6:1-11 138
8:12-25 56
11:31b 166
12:1-8 135

1 Corinthians

15:4 216

2 Corinthians

12:1-10 87

Philippians

3:7-11 102
4:10-14 85

Colossians

1:1-14 136
1:15-28 127
1:16 131

2 Thessalonians

3:13 161

1 Timothy

6:6-19 160

2 Timothy

2:15 83

Hebrews

11:3 163

James

3:18-4:3 69

1 John

4:7-12, 20-21 53

Revelation

5.11-14 40
22:1-21 84

Contributor Index

1. Connie Braun Epp. Winnipeg, Manitoba.
2. Joan Yoder Miller. Goshen, Indiana.
3. Randall Spaulding. Sarasota, Florida.
4. Karla Stoltzfus. Iowa City, Iowa.
5. Cynthia Breeze. Champaign, Illinois.
6. Jane Stoltzfus Buller. Goshen, Indiana.
7. Sherah-Leigh Gerber. Apple Creek, Ohio.
8. Beth Jarrett. Neffsville, Pennsylvania.
9. Cynthia Breeze. Urbana, Illinois.
10. Joanna Harader. Lawrence, Kansas.
11. George Dupuy. Luray, Virginia.
12. Arlyn Friesen Epp. Winnipeg, Manitoba.
13. Ruth Isaac Wiederkehr. Saskatoon, Saskatchewan.
14. Sue Nickel. Delta, British Columbia.
15. Jessica Schrock-Ringenberg. Bryan, Ohio.
16. June Mears Driedger. Lansing, Michigan.
17. Joanna Harader. Lawrence, Kansas.
18. Randall Spaulding. Sarasota, Florida.
19. Jessica Schrock-Ringenberg. Bryan, Ohio.
20. Karla Stoltzfus. Iowa City, Iowa.
21. Jane Stoltzfus Buller. Goshen, Indiana.
22. Jane Stoltzfus Buller. Goshen, Indiana.
23. Ruth Preston Schilk. Lethbridge, Alberta. *Leader*, Spring 2008.
24. John D. Rempel. Elkhart, Indiana.
25. Leslie James. Wichita, Kansas.
26. Leslie James. Wichita, Kansas.
27. E. Elaine Kauffman. Mountain Lake, Minnesota.

28. Muzet D. Felgar. Waynesboro, Virginia.
29. Ruth Isaac Wiederkehr. Saskatoon, Saskatchewan.
30. John D. Rempel. Elkhart, Indiana.
31. Jessica Schrock-Ringenberg. Bryan, Ohio.
32. Karla Stoltzfus. Iowa City, Iowa.
33. Karla Stoltzfus. Iowa City, Iowa.
34. Vernon K. Rempel. Denver, Colorado.
35. Michelle Jantzi Dueck. Winnipeg, Manitoba, *Bulletin Series*, October 19, 2008.
36. Cynthia Breeze. Urbana, Illinois.
37. Russell Mast. Walnut Creek, Ohio.
38. Samson Lo. Vancouver, British Columbia, *Bulletin Series*, May 6, 2007.
39. Tom Harder. Wichita, Kansas, *Bulletin Series*, September 30, 2007.
40. Sharon Kennel. Strang, Nebraska, *Bulletin Series*, April 22, 2007.
41. Kenneth L. Thompson. Bronx, New York, *Bulletin Series*, August 10, 2008.
42. Sylvia Shirk Charles. New York, New York, *Bulletin Series*, July 27, 2008.
43. Cynthia Breeze. Champaign, Illinois, *Bulletin Series*, July 8, 2007.
44. Ruben Chupp. Nappanee, Indiana. *Bulletin Series*. June 10, 2007.
45. Cynthia Breeze. Champaign, Illinois.
46. Lois Harder. Elkhart, Indiana, *Indiana-Michigan Worship Anthology*, 2000.
47. Lois Harder. Elkhart, Indiana, *Indiana-Michigan Worship Anthology*, 2000.
48. Michelle Jantzi Dueck. Winnipeg, Manitoba, *Bulletin Series*, July 30, 2006.
49. Michelle Jantzi Dueck. Winnipeg, Manitoba.
50. Joanna Harader. Lawrence, Kansas.
51. Doug Luginbill. Wichita, Kansas.
52. Joan Yoder Miller. Goshen, Indiana.
53. Ruth Preston Schilk. Lethbridge, Alberta.
54. Tym Elias. Winnipeg, Manitoba.
55. Vernon K. Rempel. Denver, Colorado.
56. Cynthia Breeze. Champaign, Illinois.

57. Sharon Kennel. Strang, Nebraska.
58. Arlyn Friesen Epp. Winnipeg, Manitoba.
59. Stanley W. Green. Elkhart, Indiana, *Bulletin Series,* November 7, 2007.
60. David Rogalsky. Waterloo, Ontario, *Bulletin Series,* October 15, 2006.
61. Linda Huber Mininger. Halifax, Pennsylvania, *Bulletin Series.* October 21, 2007.
62. Marlene Kropf. Elkhart, Indiana.
63. Rodger K. Schmell. Perkasie, Pennsylvania.
64. Jane Stoltzfus Buller. Goshen, Indiana.
65. Gloria Y. Diener. Harrisonburg, Virginia.
66. Joanna Harader. Lawrence, Kansas.
67. Mag Richer Smith. Iowa City, Iowa.
68. Sarah Thompson. Elkhart, Indiana, *People's Summit,* June 2008.
69. Ron Rempel. Waterloo, Ontario. *Bulletin Series.* September 24, 2006.
70. Mag Richer Smith. Iowa City, Iowa.
71. Michelle Jantzi Dueck. Winnipeg, Manitoba.
72. Karla Stoltzfus. Iowa City, Iowa.
73. Ross Ringenberg. Middlebury, Indiana.
74. Michelle Jantzi Dueck, Winnipeg, Manitoba, *Bulletin Series,* November 2, 2008.
75. Leo Hartshorn. Lancaster, Pennsylvania.
76. Bj Leichty, Wakarusa, Indiana. *Indiana-Michigan Worship Anthology,* 2000.
77. Sylvia Shirk Charles. New York, New York.
78. Lara Hall Blosser. Scottdale, Pennsylvania.
79. Barbara Krehbiel Gehring. Manhatten, Kansas.
80. Carmen Schrock-Hurst. Harrisonburg, Virginia.
81. June Mears Driedger. Lansing, Michigan.
82. Mary Mae Swartzentruber. Kitchener, Ontario.
83. Daniel P. Schrock. Goshen, Indiana.
84. Daniel P. Schrock. Goshen, Indiana.
85. Daniel P. Schrock. Goshen, Indiana.
86. Arlene Davies-Fuhr. Edmonton, Alberta.
87. Daniel P. Schrock. Goshen, Indiana.

88. Arlene Davies-Fuhr. Edmonton, Alberta.
89. Daniel P. Schrock. Goshen, Indiana.
90. Daniel P. Schrock. Goshen, Indiana.
91. Arlene Davies-Fuhr. Edmonton, Alberta.
92. Karla Stoltzfus. Iowa City, Iowa.
93. John D. Rempel. Elkhart, Indiana.
94. Joel Miller. Cincinnati, Ohio.
95. John D. Rempel. Elkhart, Indiana.
96. Jonathan P. Larson. Atlanta, Georgia.
97. Carmen Schrock-Hurst. Harrisonburg, Virginia.
98. Joel Short. Smithville, Ohio, *Indiana-Michigan Anthology*, 2000.
99. Marlin Thomas/Warren Tyson. Eastern District Conference.
100. Carmen Schrock-Hurst. Harrisonburg, Virginia
101. Jennifer Davis Sensenig. Harrisonburg, Virginia.
102. Daniel P. Schrock. Goshen, Indiana.
103. Bob Smith. Iowa City, Iowa.
104. Lois Seimens. Kerrobert, Saskatchewan.
105. Arlyn Friesen Epp. Winnipeg, Manitoba.
106. Linda Nafziger-Meiser. Boise, Idaho.
107. Jane Stoltzfus Buller. Goshen, Indiana.
108. Linda Nafziger-Meiser. Boise, Idaho.
109. Linda Nafziger-Meiser. Boise, Idaho.
110. Carmen Schrock-Hurst. Harrisonburg, Virginia.
111. Julian Forth. Chapel Hill, North Carolina.
112. Sara Dick. Newton, Kansas.
113. Arlyn Friesen Epp. Winnipeg, Manitoba.
114. Arlene Mark. Elkhart, Indiana.
115. Marlene Kropf. Elkhart, Indiana.
116. Jennifer Davis Sensenig. Harrisonburg, Virginia.
117. Marlene Kropf. Elkhart, Indiana.
118. Carmen Schrock-Hurst. Harrisonburg, Virginia.
119. Sara Dick. Newton, Kansas.
120. George Dupuy. Luray, Virginia.
121. Elsie Hannah Ruth Rempel. Winnipeg, Manitoba.
122. David Moser. Goshen, Indiana.
123. Vernon K. Rempel. Denver, Colorado.

124. Vernon K. Rempel. Denver, Colorado.

125. Arlene Mark. Elkhart, Indiana.

126. Cynthia Breeze. Champaign, Illinois.

127. Cynthia Breeze. Champaign, Illinois.

128. Mike Bogard. Newton, Kansas.

129. Jane Yoder-Short. Kalona, Iowa.

130. Patrick Preheim. Saskatoon, Saskatchewan, *Bulletin Series*, July 6, 2008.

131. Eric Massanari. Newton, Kansas, *Bulletin Series*, November 25, 2007.

132. Zulma Prieto. Goshen, Indiana, *Bulletin Series*, November 19, 2006.

133. Jessica Schrock-Ringenberg. Bryan, Ohio.

134. Ruth Preston Schilk. Lethbridge, Alberta.

135. Rachelle Lyndaker Schlabach. MCC, Washington, D.C. *Leader*, Summer 2007.

136. Cynthia Breeze. Champaign, Illinois, *Bulletin Series*, July 15, 2007.

137. Matt Friesen. Albany, Oregon, *Bulletin Series*, May 20, 2007.

138. June Galle Krehbiel. Moundridge, Kansas, *Bulletin Series*, June 22, 2008.

139. Sue Nickel. Delta, British Columbia.

140. Michelle Jantzi Dueck. Winnipeg, Manitoba, *Bulletin Series*, August 13, 2006.

141. Randall Spaulding. Sarasota, Florida.

142. Randall Spaulding. Sarasota, Florida.

143. John D. Rempel. Elkhart, Indiana.

144. Joel Miller. Cincinnati, Ohio.

145. Mag Richer Smith. Iowa City, Iowa.

146. Jerry Stutzman. Salem, Oregon.

147. Cynthia Breeze. Champaign, Illinois.

148. Muzet D. Felgar. Waynesboro, Virginia.

149. Leslie James. Wichita, Kansas.

150. Patrick Preheim. Saskatoon, Saskatchewan, *Bulletin Series*, July 13, 2008.

151. Leslie James. Wichita, Kansas.

152. Carmen Schrock-Hurst. Harrisonburg, Virginia.

153. Elaine Maust. Meridian, Mississippi.
154. Isaac S. Villegas. Chapel Hill, North Carolina.
155. St Paul Mennonite Fellowship. St Paul, Minnesota.
156. Vernon K. Rempel. Denver, Colorado.
157. Cynthia Breeze. Champaign, Illinois.
158. Cynthia Breeze. Champaign, Illinois.
159. Karla Stoltzfus. Iowa City, Iowa.
160. Isaac S. Villegas. Chapel Hill, North Carolina.
161. Eric Massanari. Newton, Kansas, *Bulletin Series*, December 18, 2007.
162. Joel Short. Smithville, Ohio, *Indiana Michigan Anthology*, 2000.
163. Terry Zimmerly. Winnipeg, Manitoba, *Bulletin Series*, August 12, 2007.
164. Terry Zimmerly. Winnipeg, Manitoba, *Bulletin Series*, August 5, 2007.
165. Verle Brubaker. Princess Anne, Maryland, *Bulletin Series*, June 1, 2008.
166. Kenneth L. Thompson. Bronx, New York, *Bulletin Series*, August 17, 2008.
167. Randall Spaulding. Sarasota, Florida.
168. James M. Lapp. Harleysville, Pennsylvania.
169. Michelle Jantzi, Anna Ruth Hershberger, and Tim Friesen. Winnipeg, Manitoba.
170. Home Street Mennonite Church. Winnipeg, Manitoba.
171. Michelle Jantzi. Winnipeg, Manitoba.
172. June Mears Driedger. Lansing, Michigan.
173. Michelle Jantzi, Anna Ruth Hershberger, and Tim Friesen. Winnipeg, Manitoba.
174. Mag Richer Smith. Iowa City, Iowa.
175. Linea Reimer Geiser. Goshen, Indiana.
176. Mag Richer Smith. Iowa City, Iowa.
177. Isaac S. Villegas. Chapel Hill, North Carolina.
178. Barbara Krehbiel Gehering. Manhatten, Kansas.
179. Connie Braun Epp. Winnipeg, Manitoba.
180. James M. Lapp. Harleysville, Pennsylvania.

181. Barbara Krehbiel Gehring. Manhatten, Kansas.
182. Mennonite Church Saskatchewan team. *Leader*, Fall 2005.
183. Michelle Jantzi Dueck. Winnipeg, Manitoba.
184. Nina B. Lanctot. Bristol, Indiana.
185. Michelle Jantzi Dueck. Winnipeg, Manitoba.
186. Michelle Jantzi Dueck. Winnipeg, Manitoba.
187. Leslie James. Wichita, Kansas.
188. George Dupuy. Luray, Virginia.
189. Cynthia Breeze. Urbana, Illinois.
190. Karla Stoltzfus. Iowa City, Iowa.
191. Karla Stoltzfus. Iowa City, Iowa.
192. George Dupuy. Luray, Virginia.
193. Michelle Jantzi Dueck. Winnipeg, Manitoba.
194. Rachel Epp Miller, San Antonio, Texas.
195. *Denominational Resources: Wanderer, Come Home,* Lent 1995.
196. *Denominational Resources: Wanderer, Come Home,* Lent 1995.
197. *Denominational Resources: Come Home to the Feast,* Lent 2001.
198. Mag Richer Smith. Iowa City, Iowa.
199. Ruth Preston Schilk. Lethbridge, Alberta.
200. *Builder: Broken and Blessed,* Lent 2000.
201. Joan Yoder Miller. *Denominational Resources,* Lent 1993.
202. *Denominational Resources: Wanderer, Come Home,* Lent 1995.
203. *Denominational Resources: Wanderer, Come Home,* Lent 1995.
204. Paul Dyck. Milverton, Ontario.
205. Arlene Mark. Elkhart, Indiana.
206. Elsie Hannah Ruth Rempel. Winnipeg, Manitoba.
207. Sara Dick. Newton, Kansas.
208. Linea Reimer Geiser. Goshen, Indiana.
209. Linea Reimer Geiser. Goshen, Indiana.
210. *Denominational resources: Lent/Holy Week/Easter* 1998.
211. Chad Mason. Des Moines, Iowa.
212. Carmen Schrock-Hurst. Harrisonburg, Virginia.

213. Randall Spaulding. Sarasota, Florida.
214. Patty and Tim Peebles. Chicago, Illinois.
215. Julie Prey-Harbaugh. Philadelphia, Pennsylvania.
216. Mary Mae Swartzentruber. Kitchener, Ontario.
217. George Dupuy. Luray, Virginia.
218. Thomas Lees. Chapel Hill, North Carolina.
219. Tym Elias. Winnipeg, Manitoba.
220. Tym Elias. Winnipeg, Manitoba.
221. *Leader*, Spring 2008.
222. Lois Siemens. Kerrobert, Saskatchewan.
223. John D. Rempel. Elkhart, Indiana.
224. George Dupuy. Luray, Virginia.
225. Chad Mason. Des Moines, Iowa.
226. Ruth Preston Schilk. Lethbridge, Alberta, *Leader*, Spring 2008.
227. Lois Siemens. Kerrobert, Saskatchewan, *Vision Journal*, Spring 2005.
228. George Dupuy. Luray, Virginia.
229. Linea Reimer Geiser. Goshen, Indiana, *Purpose*, May 1988.
230. Jennifer Davis Sensenig. Harrisonburg, Virginia.
231. Matt Friesen. Albany, Oregon, *Bulletin Series*, May 27, 2007.
232. Matt Friesen. Albany, Oregon, *Bulletin Series*, May 27, 2007
233. Leslie James. Wichita, Kansas.
234. Leslie James. Wichita, Kansas.
235. Leslie James. Wichita, Kansas.
236. Vernon K. Rempel. Denver, Colorado.
237. John D. Rempel. Elkhart, Indiana.
238. David P. Conrad. Washington, D.C.
239. David P. Conrad. Washington, D.C.
240. Elaine Maust. Meridian, Mississippi.
241. Linda Nafziger-Meiser. Boise, Idaho.
242. Russell Mast. Walnut Creek, Ohio.
243. Linda Nafziger-Meiser. Boise, Idaho.
244. Connie Braun Epp. Winnipeg, Manitoba.
245. Linda Nafziger-Meiser. Boise, Idaho.
246. Marlene Kropf. Elkhart, Indiana.

247. Elaine Maust. Meridian, Mississippi.
248. Linda Nafziger-Meiser. Boise, Idaho.
249. Linda Nafziger-Meiser. Boise, Idaho.
250. Marlene Kropf. Elkhart, Indiana.
251. Dan Miller. Goshen, Indiana, *Indiana Michigan Anthology*, 2000.
252. Nancy Kauffmann. Goshen, Indiana, *Indiana Michigan Anthology*, 2001.
253. Scott Bergen. Winnipeg, Manitoba.
254. Linda Nafziger-Meiser. Boise, Idaho.
255. Vernon K. Rempel. Denver, Colorado.
256. June Mears Driedger. Lansing, Michigan.
257. Elaine Maust. Meridian, Mississippi.
258. Gloria Y. Diener. Harrisonburg, Virginia.
259. Joan Yoder Miller. Goshen, Indiana.
260. Carmen Schrock-Hurst. Harrisonburg, Virginia. *PeaceSigns* e-magazine.
261. Doug Luginbill. Wichita, Kansas.
262. Rod Stafford. Portland, Oregon.
263. David Moser. Goshen, Indiana.
264. Rod Stafford. Portland, Oregon.
265. Vernon K. Rempel. Denver, Colorado.
266. Esther Lanting. Wakarusa, Indiana, *Indiana Michigan Anthology*, 2001.
267. Sue Clemmer Steiner. Waterloo, Ontario, *Symposium on Worship*, May 1996.
268. Vernon K. Rempel. Denver, Colorado.
269. Jonathan P. Larson. Atlanta, Georgia.
270. Michael Bogard. Newton, Kansas.
271. Carmen Schrock-Hurst. Harrisonburg, Virginia.
272. Sue Clemmer Steiner. Waterloo, Ontario, *Symposium on Worship,* May 1996.
273. Esther Lanting. Wakarusa, Indiana.
274. Carmen Schrock-Hurst. Harrisonburg, Virginia.
275. Jessica Schrock-Ringenberg. Bryan, Ohio.
276. Leslie James. Wichita, Kansas.
277. Willmar T. Harder. Inman, Kansas.
278. Karla Stoltzfus. Iowa City, Iowa.

279. Karla Stoltzfus. Iowa City, Iowa.
280. Carmen Schrock-Hurst. Harrisonburg, Virgina.
281. Jessica Schrock-Ringenberg. Bryan, Ohio.
282. Carmen Schrock-Hurst. Harrisonburg, Virgina.
283. Esther Lanting. Wakarusa, Indiana, *Indiana Michigan Anthology*, 2000.
284. Elaine Maust. Meridian, Mississippi.
285. Pastor Romero. Paso Robles, California, *Indiana Michigan Anthology*, 2000.
286. Jane Yoder-Short. Kalona, Iowa.
287. Waterloo North Mennonite Church, Waterloo, Ontario.
288. Sara Dick, Newton, Kansas.
289. Shari Miller Wagner, Indianapolis, Indiana, *Indiana Michigan Anthology*, 2000.
290. Sue Clemmer Steiner. Waterloo, Ontario.
291. Linda Nafziger-Meiser. Boise, Idaho.
292. Linda Nafziger-Meiser. Boise, Idaho.
293. Linda Nafziger-Meiser. Boise, Idaho.
294. Lethbridge (Alberta) Mennonite Church.
295. Waterloo North (Ontario) Mennonite Church.
296. Myrna Miller Dyck. Baden, Ontario.
297. James M. Lapp. Harleysville, Pennsylvania.
298. Joel Short. Smithville, Ohio, *Indiana Michigan Anthology*, 2000.
299. Nina Bartelt Lanctot. Bristol, Indiana, *Indiana Michigan Anthology*, 2000.
300. James M. Lapp. Harleysville, Pennsylvania.
301. Ed Kauffman. Sioux Falls, South Dakota.
302. Linda Lefever Alley. Harrisonburg, Virginia.
303. St. Jacobs (Ontario) Mennonite Church, 1995.
304. Cynthia Breeze. Champaign, Illinois, *Jubilee Publications*.
305. Miriam Zehr. Orville, Ohio.
306. Arlyn Friesen Epp. Winnipeg, Manitoba.
307. Waterloo (Ontario) North Mennonite Church.
308. Eric Massanari. Newton, Kansas, *Leader*, Fall 2005.
309. Jane Roeschley. Normal, Illinois.
310. Lynette Wiebe. Winnipeg, Manitoba.

311. Marlene Kropf. Elkhart, Indiana.
312. Marlene Kropf. Elkhart, Indiana.
313. Mag Richer Smith. Iowa City, Iowa.
314. Marlene Kropf. Elkhart, Indiana.
315. John D. Rempel. Elkhart, Indiana.
316. *Denominational resources*, 1999.
317. Jane Roeschley. Normal, Illinois.
318. Assembly Mennonite Church. Goshen, Indiana.
319. Connie Braun Epp. Winnipeg, Manitoba.
320. Marlene Kropf. Elkhart, Indiana.
321. Marlene Kropf. Elkhart, Indiana.

The Editor

Diane Zaerr Brenneman has
served as pastor, teacher, adminis-
trator, and denominational official
in Mennonite Church USA. She
currently moderates Central
Plains Mennonite Conference,
preaches, writes, and offers spiritual direction while also farming
alongside her husband Doug near
Wellman, Iowa.

She is a graduate of McCormick Theological Seminary, Chicago
(DMin executive leadership); Associated Mennonite Biblical
Seminary, Elkhart, Indiana (MDiv in pastoral ministry); and
Eastern Mennonite University, Harrisonburg, Virginia (BA in
elementary education). In her ministry, she has served as pastor
at First Mennonite Church of Iowa City, Iowa, and as denominational minister working with the ministerial calling system for
Mennonite Church USA. She has also served as AMBS associate
dean for continuing education, and taught elementary and middle school in two states.

Diane and Doug, along with children Maureen and Brent,
attend West Union Mennonite Church near Parnell, Iowa.